Brassey's *History of Uniforms*

Brassey's *History of Uniforms*

Barbarian Warriors

Saxons, Vikings, Normans

By Dan and Susanna Shadrake

Colour plates by Richard Hook

Series editor Tim Newark

To the members of Britannia.

First English Edition 1997

UK editorial offices: Brassey's Ltd, 33 John Street, London
WC1N 2AT
UK Orders: Marston Book Services, PO Box 269, Abingdon,
OX14 4SD

North American Orders: Brassey's Inc,
PO Box 960, Herndon, VA 22070, USA

Library of Congress Cataloging in Publication Data available
British Library Cataloguing in Publication Data
A catalogue record for this book is available from the British
Library

ISBN 1 85753 213 9 Hardcover

Typeset by Harold Martin & Redman Ltd.
Originated, printed and bound in Singapore
under the supervisison of M.R.M. Graphics Ltd,
Winslow, Buckinghamshire.

Contents

Introduction

The aim of this book is to describe in detail the military equipment of a succession of peoples who inhabited these islands between the end of the Roman Empire and the Norman Conquest, and test the credibility and effectiveness of their original equipment by reference to its present day re-enactment and recreation, not just by *Britannia*, the re-enactment group to which the authors belong, but by other specialist individuals and societies in their chosen eras. Obviously there are areas which remain uncovered to date, but the theme of this book is that it is possible and even desirable to apply the practical considerations of the military world through the Dark Ages by means of what we like to think of as reconstructive analysis.

The chapter distinctions are cultural rather than chronological, as we believe this serves to highlight the similarities between the warrior cultures which had a significant impact on the development of Britain following its independence from Roman rule. The emphasis is on re-enactment because this is a relatively new way of approaching the well trodden paths of ancient military research. Also we have sought to draw attention to the parallels between the surviving evidence and the practical lessons learnt in the field.

We would like to point out that the reconstructed items of armour and equipment in this book are in many cases speculative, but as our knowledge of history changes almost daily with the advent of new finds it can be risky to make any hard and fast rules about specific equipment and often the safest option is to present equipment and the way it was worn as interpretations. The quality of craftsmanship and attention to detail displayed by most armourers and craftspeople who service this growing side of the heritage industry deserves recognition; although there are too many highly skilled people and professional societies to include in one book, they can be seen practicing their craft at most heritage events throughout the summer months. We are attempting to put under one roof, as it were, a small portion of the wealth of detail and experience which we have encountered in the world of re-enactment and to marry it up with the historical background, thus hopefully bringing new arguments and fresh insights into a barbarian world. The use of the contentious word barbarian in the title of this book is indicative of the fact that all the cultures in this period, including the Normans, were heavily influenced by the Celtic/Germanic cultures of northern Europe. They were perceived very much as outsiders assaulting stable societies and thus deserving of the Latin eptithet barbarian, particularly when described by chroniclers living among the remains of the Roman Empire.

Opposite.

Later Roman soldier. By the 5th century a large proportion of the Roman army were of Germanic origin. (*Britannia*, reconstruction by Ted Batterham, Ian Burridge, Mandy Turner).

Lynne Smith.

Arthurian Warriors

To define the Arthurian era we must first go back to its roots in late Roman Britain. Very roughly, we are talking about a span of nearly two hundred years from 400A.D. to 600A.D. Since this is clearly more than a lifespan, we should emphasise that the era is necessarily extended to take account of the inadvisability of limiting the existence of Arthur to specific dates, although there tends to be a polarising of popular belief that an Arthur figure, *a dux bellorum*, or war leader, was prominent around 500A.D.

Since there is a dearth of specifically identifiable Arthurian militaria, the researcher/re-enactor is forced to fall back on the evidence for weapons and armour at the tail end of the Roman administration in Britain, whether it be of Roman, Celtic, Germanic or mixed origin. At the risk of repetition, the thinking behind this is that the Arthurian era did not spring from nothing; its culture is the culture of the peoples who inhabited Britain at that time, and to say they were diverse is somewhat of an understatement. However, the main influence which preceded the Britain of Arthur was that of Rome, provincial Rome maybe, but Roman nonetheless even in its military outlook and equipping. The later Roman Empire provides the material with which Arthurian Britain can be tentatively constructed.

To set the scene, most serving soldiers in Britain in the last decade of Roman rule were unlikely to have been pure Roman; rather, they would probably have been drawn from any or all of the subject peoples of the Empire including British, Germanic, North African, Greek, and Eastern nations. However, they shared a common military tradition imposed by the state of *Pax Romana*, although this was wearing a bit thin by the end of the fourth century, and the Roman love of uniformity and order was breaking down in the face of pressure from increasing barbarian influences both inside and outside the army. To appreciate the Roman military machine in its fourth century context it must be remembered that the combined effect in the previous century of the continued barbarian onslaughts on the Rhine and Danube frontiers and divisive internal struggles had placed the Empire on the defensive, an unusual position for Rome to be in, particularly after centuries of absolute confidence.

The Roman war machine found itself having to be imitative rather than innovative; having been almost self sufficient in military ability it came to rely heavily on barbarian manpower, and the province of Britain was no exception to this rule. This then is the setting for Arthur's Britain, a place where slightly out of date Roman military equipment and customs mingled with inherited native British weaponry and tribal loyalties, where imported luxury items were as much coveted and prized as the brooches of the Germanic *foederati*, and where all these items in time lost their alien identity and merged into British style. It is important to remember that the Roman withdrawal did not turn the former province of Britain into a backwater overnight; there is plenty of evidence to suggest that trade continued and thrived well into the fifth century and beyond in some favoured parts of Britain. Indeed though many fled the Romanised towns and cities to return to and fortify the hillforts of their ancestors they still maintained trade links even in the Celtic hinterlands.

It is a truism that British history started with the Roman invasion, fell silent at the end of Roman rule and resumed with the Norman invasion. Britain's and Europe's missing centuries have been subject to the most inaccurate representations in the subsequent centuries at the hands of chroniclers, artists, sculptors, the theatre and more recently film makers. At the heart of the matter is the question mark hanging over the 5th century; the answer, if found, would be the lynchpin for the next few centuries, and one of the main aims of *Britannia*, the re-enactment society, has been to establish a convincing bridge between ancient and medieval worlds in re-enactment and living history terms.

There is a commonly held belief that re-enactors who choose to portray the darkest of dark ages, between the late 4th to late 6th centuries in Britain, are motivated partly, if not solely, by the absence of detailed information in many crucial areas of equipment reconstruction – since no one knows for certain, criticism can be neatly evaded. At least that is the asssumption. The truth, however, is a different matter. Unlike their counterparts in both earlier and later periods, *Britannia* and associated groups do not enjoy the benefit of established knowledge based on a fund of accumulated and tested archaeological evidence, nor has the Arthurian era the high academic profile to attract serious and prolonged research. Indeed, in the authors' opinion, it may be suffering from the wrong kind of attention due to mystical fringe elements which deflect the genuine enquirers. But happily, since *Britannia's* foundation there has been a marked increase in enthusiasm for the authentic 5th century or Arthurian scenario, by re-enactors, the general public and heritage authorities, who have all responded to the call of a time when so many peoples and cultures met and struggled in a small forgotten island on the outer edge of the dying western Roman empire. Re-enactors of the 4th to 6th centuries do not have the advantage of being able to base assumptions about weapons, armour and equipment on the weight of documents, let alone archaeological references. What information there is, is sparse and often very well concealed, scattered in unlikely places and obscured by the misconceptions of later centuries. Re-enactors who hope to present an authentic view of this awkward but exciting period are therefore walking an uncomfortable tightrope, trying to hold their balance between a deficit of hard facts and informed reconstruction, the latter being at times the only method of resolving problems arising from gaps in current knowledge. This somewhat unorthodox solution will be discussed in greater depth later in this chapter; it is sufficient to say at this stage that *Britannia* has had to cast its nets wider than the confines of one century and further than the shores of Britain in order to amass enough data for a reasonably accurate picture of the diversity that must surely have existed in this turbulent time.

We have sought to build a convincing body of evidence for weapons, armour, clothing and equipment of the time using information from such disparate sources as the *Notitia Dignitatum* (a later Roman military document), later and post Roman writers such as Vegetius and Procopius and, closer to home, Aneirin's *Y Gododdin* (an heroic 6th century battle poem). Pictorial evidence in the form of wall

Recreated late Roman heavy infantry/cavalryman wearing a Sassanian style helmet and scale armour. Helmet by Ted Batterham, Scale armour by Matt Shadrake. Mike Brown, English Heritage.

paintings such as those in the Via Latina in Rome have been helpful; sculptural and numismatic references have also played their part, for example the Arch of the Tetrarchs in Venice, and more recently the 4th/5th century Hoxne hoard from Suffolk. Although the more visual references are not reliable because of the 'classical' tendencies of later Roman artisans, they are still valuable provided that the fanciful elements are filtered out; this is best done by using whatever archaeological parallels exist for comparison. For example, we know that the helmet depicted in the wall painting of a 4th century A.D. soldier at Via Maria Catacomb in Syracuse is not just an artist's flight of fancy even though it is shown as gilded, crested and with a frontal eye pattern because an actual example (ungilded) has been found at Intercisa in Hungary. Without that real life parallel, the rather exaggerated crest might have been dismissed as artistic licence or borrowing from classical convention. This is a method that has helped *Britannia* on more than one occasion to build a strong and varied equipment list.

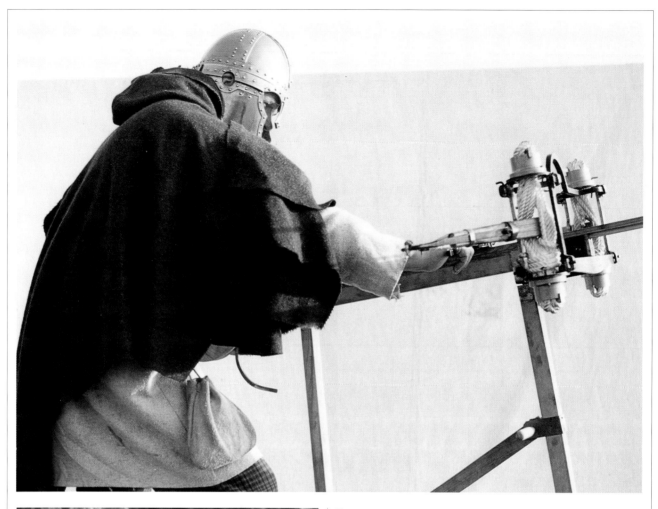

Top.

Reconstructed *Carroballista*, iron framed later Roman artillery piece used by *Britannia* (made by Bernard Jacobs).

Left.

Early Roman infantryman (*Legio VIII Augusta*). Jeff Brimble.

Archaeological evidence, despite being so rare, is still by far the best and safest reference for reconstructive purposes, but unfortunately, to find the missing elements of kit we are often obliged to look abroad. This approach is somewhat controversial, as the practical limits to comparisons between Britain and the continent in this era obviously vary according to the subject matter. The indications are that there were many similarities in military and civil life up to, and for at least a generation after the collapse of the western Roman administration; few dispute this fact, but what creates the most heated argument is the endurance of Britain's Roman identity particularly with regards to its military society. The evidence is that the large scale manufacturing base wound down and military along with trade networks were damaged to such an extent that what military society remained, especially in Britain, relied heavily on a kind of cottage industry of smiths, weavers, carpenters etc to meet the

The *Carrobalista's* velocity and range can be adjusted for use at battle re-enactments. Derek Clow.

requirements of Romano-British and (later on) Germanic warlords. Each single piece of later Roman equipment was potentially subject to all kinds of treatment, from simple repairs to the most intricate embellishment, and the replacement of major components where worn, lost, broken or discarded in favour of newer fashion; in some cases direct copying was carried out. Nowhere is this metamorphosis more evident than in the Sutton Hoo burial in East Anglia, where a richly decorated helmet of a Saxon king is clearly based on a later Roman 'Ridge' helmet. Even the early Vendel culture in Sweden betrays some later Roman foundations in its military equipment, the ubiquitous 'Ridge' helmets bearing witness to this cultural cross-pollination.

We are always alert to the discovery of new 4th century sites in Britain as any one find on one site alone could prove to be the missing piece of the puzzle. Examples of fresh evidence of 4th century (and later) activity are the recently excavated Romano-British port at Heybridge, Essex, apparently abandoned in the 5th century, and the tentatively identified cathedral, possibly commissioned by Magnus Maximus, located close to Tower Hill underground station. The search for a rich seam of later Roman reference goes on, and there is always the enticing possiblity of stumbling across some concrete evidence for the existence and endeavours of an 'Arthur'. For *Britannia*, that would be a bonus.

Cavalry

It is often argued that the distribution of named Arthurian 'battle' sites throughout Britain points towards the use of a highly mobile fast strike cavalry force. Indeed the Roman road network, which would

Fire bolt head from Dura Europos (the hollow was thought to have contained flammable material). Dan Shadrake.

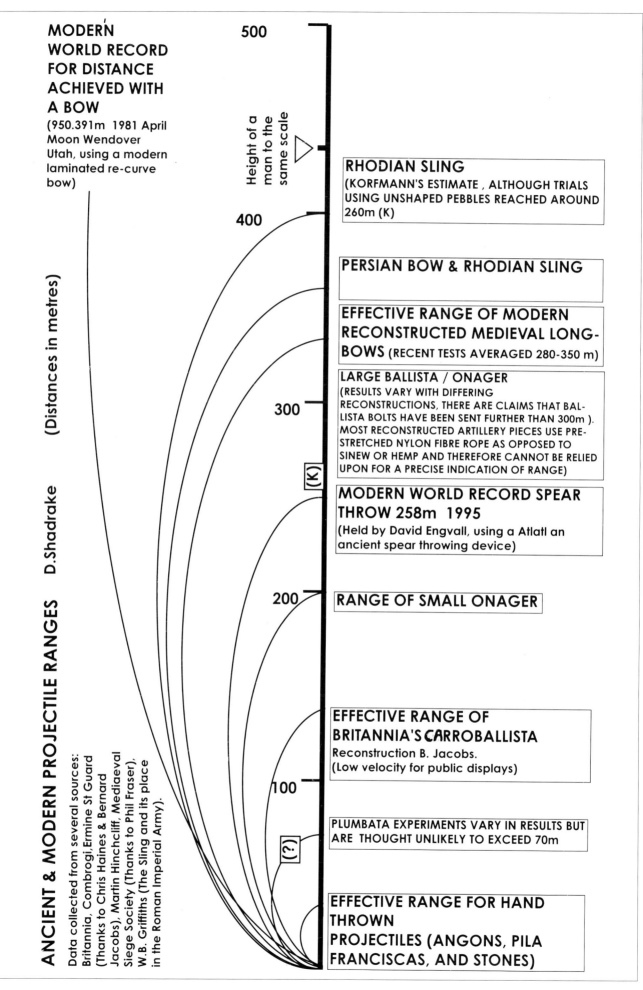

ANCIENT & MODERN PROJECTILE RANGES   D.Shadrake   (Distances in metres)

Data collected from several sources: Britannia, Combrogi, Ermine St Guard (Thanks to Chris Haines & Bernard Jacobs), Martin Hinchcliff, Mediaeval Siege Society (Thanks to Phil Fraser), W.B. Griffiths (The Sling and its place in the Roman Imperial Army).

MODERN WORLD RECORD FOR DISTANCE ACHIEVED WITH A BOW
(950.391m 1981 April Moon Wendover Utah, using a modern laminated re-curve bow)

Height of a man to the same scale

500

400

300

200

100

[K]

[?]

RHODIAN SLING
(KORFMANN'S ESTIMATE , ALTHOUGH TRIALS USING UNSHAPED PEBBLES REACHED AROUND 260m (K)

PERSIAN BOW & RHODIAN SLING

EFFECTIVE RANGE OF MODERN RECONSTRUCTED MEDIEVAL LONG-BOWS (RECENT TESTS AVERAGED 280-350 m)

LARGE BALLISTA / ONAGER
(RESULTS VARY WITH DIFFERING RECONSTRUCTIONS, THERE ARE CLAIMS THAT BALLISTA BOLTS HAVE BEEN SENT FURTHER THAN 300m). MOST RECONSTRUCTED ARTILLERY PIECES USE PRE-STRETCHED NYLON FIBRE ROPE AS OPPOSED TO SINEW OR HEMP AND THEREFORE CANNOT BE RELIED UPON FOR A PRECISE INDICATION OF RANGE)

MODERN WORLD RECORD SPEAR THROW 258m 1995
(Held by David Engvall, using a Atlatl an ancient spear throwing device)

RANGE OF SMALL ONAGER

EFFECTIVE RANGE OF BRITANNIA'S CARROBALLISTA
Reconstruction B. Jacobs.
(Low velocity for public displays)

PLUMBATA EXPERIMENTS VARY IN RESULTS BUT ARE THOUGHT UNLIKELY TO EXCEED 70m

EFFECTIVE RANGE FOR HAND THROWN PROJECTILES (ANGONS, PILA FRANCISCAS, AND STONES)

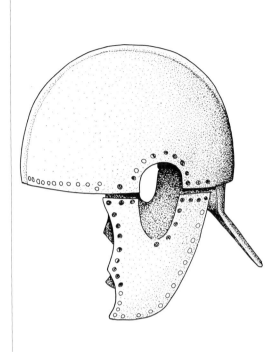

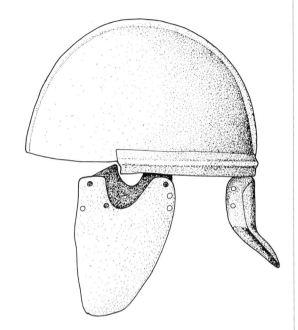

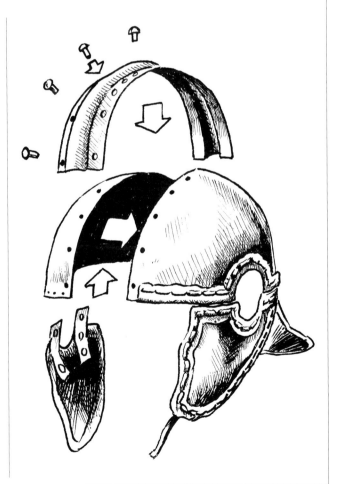

have been in good condition even after some years of neglect, would have been an efficient and swift means of moving cavalry, whether heavy or light, throughout Britain. We have no direct evidence in the form of archaeological finds that an Arthurian cavalry was operational, yet bearing in mind the province of Britain had been a strong importer of equine blood-stock, such as Frisian cavalry mounts, it seems likely that such a strong tradition of cavalry combined with native Celtic affinity with horses would not wither away but would be put to good use. The figure of Arthur is credited with being an outstanding military commander; such a commander would use any advantage to gain ground over his enemy. Therefore if we subscribe to Arthur's use of cavalry then we can conjecture that the mounts (and of their size and type we know nothing) would be equipped with inherited

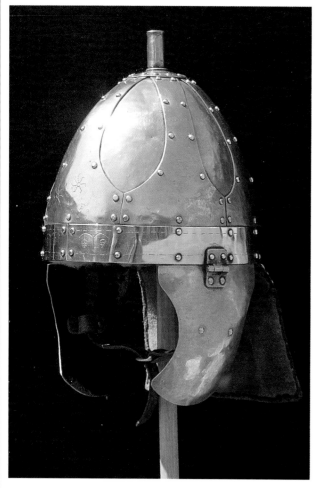

late Roman military horse gear; in particular the four-horned saddle as reconstructed by Peter Connolly shows how the Roman and then later Arthurian cavalryman could have kept himself in the saddle without stirrups despite the strenuous exertions of battle, maintaining a secure seat both in combat and on heavy impacts. It seems perfectly feasible that a strong tradition of horse warfare would retain such a saddle if it had proved its worth.

Artillery

A definite advantage of extending the time limits of *Britannia's* 'catchment area' to include re-enactment of the later Roman army before the watershed of 410 A.D. is that one can rely on the last years of order and organisation to source the group with items of living history equipment and hardware not normally associated with Dark Age societies. The most obvious

Left.

Replica of a *spangenhelm,* made by Ivor Lawton, *Dawn of Time Crafts.*

Bottom.

Ivor and Simone Lawton of *Dawn of Time* Crafts, re-creating the type of smiths and craftspeople that would have served the warlords of Arthurian Britain.

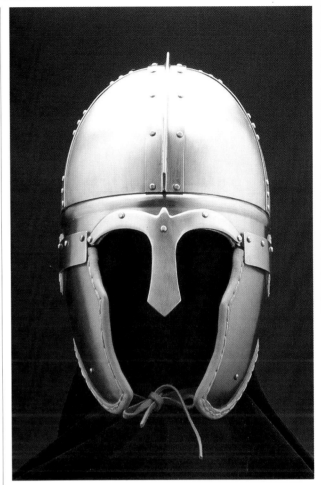

Top.
Interpretations of the Burgh Castle helmet, made by Ivor
Lawton, *Dawn of Time Crafts*.

Right.
Recreated Infantryman in basic ridge or 'Sassanian' helmet.
Matt Shadrake.

is the acquisition of a *carroballista* (cart or wall mounted bolt throwing device); this iron-framed later Roman artillery piece is based on several surviving components from Orsova and Gornea (Romania). This category of artefact (found in Roman military sites abandoned in the 4th century) roughly conformed to the Roman writer Heron's description of the *cheiroballista* and Vegetius' description of the *manuballista*: 'They used to call scorpions what are now called manuballistae (hand catapults) they were so named because they inflicted death with tiny thin darts' (Vegetius Book IV).

The surviving components are from an iron framed machine (which is a little too large to be a hand held device) and are part of an iron structure that includes a frame for supporting the springs of rope or sinew cord (of which two were needed). These components were made from two solid rings joined together by two

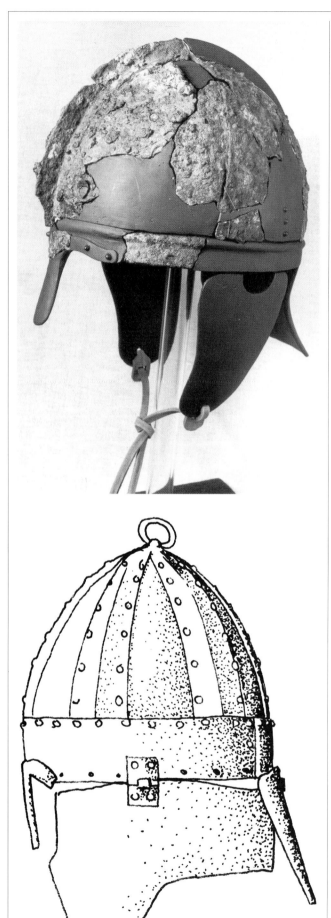

struts of equal thickness (this component was referred to by Heron as the *kambestrion*). Both these struts have lugs which face outwards and are obviously intended to receive the single iron cross piece (or Heron's *kamerion*) of which one example survives. This crosspiece has a round arch in the centre and it has been suggested that this was used as a device for aim or range (see *Gudea und Baatz Teile Spatromischer Ballisten aus Gornea und Orsova Rumanien*, 1974). According to Heron the third major component of the iron frame was the *klimekion* which was an iron ladder-shaped item that also connected to the twin frames of the torsion cylinders below the *kamerion* or cross piece. No archaeological examples of the *klimekion* survive, but enough visual and literary data exists from

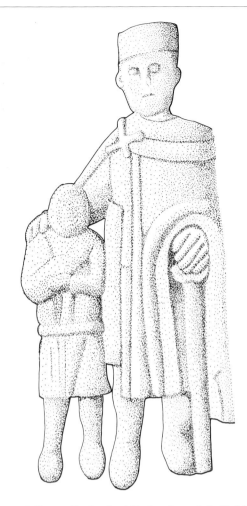

Representation on the tomb of Flavius Augustalis (Italy), depictions of soldiers and civilians in Pannonian or 'Pill-box' hats are common throughout the areas covered by the Roman Empire. Iain Bell.

Reconstruction of *Flavius Augustalis* by G. Lee, M. Turner. Lynne Smith.

which to make a servicable reconstruction. The iron frame was thought to have been a late Empire improvement to an already efficient weapon, as iron would not have been prone to warping unlike even the great oak and ash frames of the earlier 'Hellenistic' style machines. The images of small twin torsion ballistas on the Trajan's column relief carving show similar components to the Gornea and Orsova artefacts. The raised arch on the cross piece (or *kamerion*) is represented here as a little exaggerated and the twisted cord springs and their supporting frames (*kambestria*) appear to be enclosed in cylinders, which may have been copper alloy or leather covers against the elements. Alternatively, there is the proposal that the torsion springs were not covered by cylinders but left open. This school of thought subscribes to the theory that the twisted cord torsions were once represented on Trajan's column with paint which has since worn off the surface of this relief, giving the impression of smooth cylinders. This latter theory (that the torsion cords were exposed) was

considered the best option for reconstruction when *Britannia* commissioned its own modest *carroballista* from B. Jacobs (specialist in ancient torsion engines). The lack of archaeological examples of these cylinders was the deciding factor in leaving the cord springs exposed.

The range of re-enactment artillery pieces cannot

Holes in the rim of some surviving ridge helmets may indicate rawhide edging. This takes considerably less effort and skill to do than applying a metal edge. Dan Shadrake.

Top.
Anti-Cavalry Formation, *Britannia* **at the Heybridge archaeological site.** (E.C.C)

Left.
Shield under construction.

always be relied on as a precise indicator of the range of the original; the choice of modern rope made from artificial fibres is necessary in most cases, as the cost and difficulties in obtaining and maintaining horsehair or sinew torsion springs is beyond the means of most modern re-enactment and living history societies. Reconstructed bolts are based on examples found as far apart as Vindolanda (Hadrian's Wall), Caerleon (South Wales), and Dura Europos (Syria). The *carroballista* and other such devices can be said with certainty to be relevant to 4th and 5th century military life in Britain; in particular the South and East coasts where their massive, imposing stone forts were ideal housing for this type of artillery, with their towers providing perfect platforms for these weapons. One of the forts of this Saxon Shore defence line, Burgh Castle or *Garrianonum* (perhaps one of the best preserved examples) boasts circular towers with centrally placed socket holes in the top of each one, which it has been suggested are firing platforms for such artillery. Having visited the site, we can see this proposal as quite realistic, as the towers command an excellent view of marshland (what would have been a wide inlet or bay in the later Roman era) and flat arable land surrounding its surviving land facing walls. Such a weapon would have been an effective deterrent against raiders considering its range and accuracy (our reconstruction has sent a 6 inch bolt with an iron head through a 10mm plywood shield up to its wooden flights at a range of 60 metres). The maximum range of this device in experiments is 140 metres (using torsion springs made from artificial fibre). Large *ballistae* reconstructions have recorded ranges of just over 300 metres; the devastating power of the *ballistae* is further attested by Vegetius when he refers to '*ballista* bolts which no cuirass or shield can withstand'. Whilst *Britannia* has no problem with exhibiting this

Right.

Colour designs applied to a the shield's surface of wet chalk on fabric, a natural range of oil paints were used to simulate ancient pigments. Dan Shadrake.

Bottom.

Line up of assorted shields reconstructed by Jeff Brimble. Legio VIII Augusta.

20 Arthurian Warriors

Top.
Two finds of scale armour from Britain, the small scales on the right are 'tinned' copper alloy scales found in Chester. The large cluster on the left is lamellar from the Somerset levels. The British Museum.

Right.
Shields in re-enactment are often faced with hessian, painted and edged with rawhide to protect their wooden surfaces against blows. These measures can extend the field 'life' of a shield by months, even years. Dan Shadrake.

device in the role of later Roman *limitanei* or static local troops, trying to employ it in a British setting further than a lifetime from the 410 A.D. benchmark would create a great deal of tiresome controversy. There is certainly little evidence that engines of war had any significant impact on British problems after this date; the 4th-6th century accounts of Britain are vague in this context and seeing that Gildas and Nennius have been subjected to more than a little

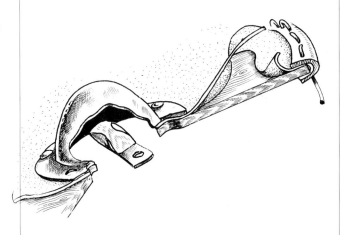

Opposite.
Leather hide lamellar, reconstruction by Gary Foreland (the helmet is an amalgam of several 6th century Scandinavian and British examples).

Late Roman officer / Arthurian Warrior, c. 450 A.D.

The helmet worn by the main figure is an interpretation of the 'Burgh Castle' helmet. This style of headgear is referred to as a heavy Sassanian or 'Heavy Ridge' helmet and is based on the dome found at Burgh Castle in Norfolk, England. There are several parallels of this helmet on the continent and most surviving examples tend to be richly decorated in either silver or gilded skins and are often inlaid with glass or semi-precious stones.

The top left-hand helmet is referred to as the light Sassanian or 'Light Ridge' helmet, examples of this helmet have been found throughout Europe; fragments of an iron helmet bowl found at Richborough in Kent would suggest its use in a British context. This representation is based on the example found at Intercisa in Hungary, the exact significance of the eye pattern is not known. Surviving helmets of the Light Ridge type were rarely decorated to the degree that the Heavy Ridge helmets were.

The helmet below the Light Ridge is the Der el Medineh helmet, this is a *Spangenhelm* or segmented helmet found in Egypt. It was composed of metal segments supported by metal struts rivetted to a browband. No definite examples of later Roman or Saxon era spangenhelms occur in Britain, but the frequency of finds in Europe and artistic representations on the continent and indeed Britain would suggest that it would be unreasonable to exclude it from a British context.

The uppermost sword is based on the surviving British and continental examples of Germanic style swords, the blades are of the long parallel sided spatha style but the hilts are typical of the Frankish or Saxon styles of the 4th-7th centuries and represent a transitional stage of sword development from the classical to the medieval. This is based on the Feltwell sword from the Norfolk/Suffolk Border. The middle sword hilt is a representation of the Koln *spatha*, this example's hilt was carved entirely from ivory but modern reconstructions tend to use synthetic resin or hardwoods. The bottom sword is an amalgam of several late and sub Roman finds, the cross-guard is metal and based on one of the spathas from the 4th century Nydam boat burial in Denmark. The stylised grip is of spiral carved bone and based on a 3rd-4th century German find from Buch in Germany, the pommel is also based on a carved bone

type from Germany (Zugmantel). This sword is represented on the main figure as suspended in a leather scabbard from a highly decorated baldric (after M.C. Bishop & J.C.N. Coulston, *Roman Military Equipment),* this is typical of the style of sword carrying depicted on many later Roman artistic representations and archaeological finds (Corbridge, Zugmantel, Dura Europos).

The main figure wears a cuirass of 'Lamellar' armour, this is a form of scale armour that developed in the East and was thought to have migrated into the Roman Empire sometime in the 3rd century A.D. Lamellar, unlike conventional scale armour needs no backing fabric or leather garment as the scales are self-supporting (each scale is laced to its horizontal and vertical neighbours, and modern re-constructions show that this lacing helps do disperse blows). The bottom right hand illustration of the reverse lacing pattern of lamellar is a slight mis-representation.

The conventional scale armour represented here is based on the example found at Carpow in Perthshire, these tiny copper alloy scales (1cm) were linked to each other in horizontal rows by means of wire rings, these rows were then fixed to a fabric backing by stitches that ran through holes in the top of each scale and were secured to a leather thong. Ringmail was used throughout the Roman era and the Dark Ages. Roman mail was made of alternating rows of solid wire and riveted links. Re-enactors often use spring-washers or joined wire links (represented here by the artist).

The serpent standard or 'Draco' was adopted by the Roman army from the Sarmatians sometime in the 3rd century A.D. This type of battle standard worked on the hollow windsock principal (filling with air and fluttering in the wind). Artistic representation suggests that this type of battle standard continued to be used by the Saxons well into the 11th century.

The weapons illustrated at the bottom are the *spiculum* or throwing spear, possibly the type described by Vegetius, the lead weighted throwing dart or *plumbata* and the spear or *lancea*. The oval shield was likely to have been edged with rawhide by this time and the shield pattern is based on the *Secundani Britanniorum,* a Roman unit based on the South and East coasts of Britain according to the *Notitia Dignitatum,* a later Roman document dated to the early 5th century.

Painting by Richard Hook.

'mediaeval editing', any hint of such devices must be regarded with extreme caution, also the quite prolific British bolt head finds are rather ambiguous as they could just as easily be light javelin heads with provenance from any point in the Roman occupation. An interesting bolt head was found at Dura Europos; this was made from three bars that extended from their socket head which bowed outwards and back in to the single point of the bolt head. This 'bowing out'

forms a cage into which flammable material could be inserted and would certainly match the type of fire dart described by Ammianus Marcellinus. Five Roman arrowheads manufactured in the same way were discovered at Bar hill in Scotland and varied in length from 5.2 – 6cm. The operating and maintenance skills required for both the *ballista* and the *onager* (large stone thrower) could be easily passed on, but the inevitable wear and tear on specific components would

Close up of a section of medieval European ringmail, (the large stamped alloy ring is the maker's mark). Half the rings are solid loops, whereas the other have been riveted. Royal Armouries, Tower of London.

mean that the existing 'cottage industry' could not cope with repairs, and it must also be safe to assume that people evacuating an area in a hurry would not be able to transport such war engines easily (it is difficult enough even with the advantages of modern vehicles). However, this begs the question of whether such engines would in any case be in the possession of non-military locals following the decay and demise of the Saxon Shore forts and their inland equivalents. The authors think it highly unlikely that they would have continued to exist in a cohesive military context for longer than a generation. Of course, there may have been isolated exceptions with specific geographical advantages. The general picture, in our opinion, is one of opportunist applications by isolated entrepreneurial warlords within tribal territories, rather than a home guard defence.

Military Camps

Our other major item of later and indeed post Roman military camp life is a single unit tent, but despite surviving fragments of tents found in Britain at Vindolanda, Newstead and Segontium we have nothing specifically from the late or post Roman era except some rather interesting 5th century Byzantine Hellenistic style miniatures, depicting scenes from the *Iliad*. Having no archaeological references himself, the eastern Roman artist who executed the miniatures has based several military scenes on his own era rather than ancient Greece, so that whilst there may be some elements that are deliberately classical the overall picture is without doubt late Roman in appearance. Two distinct tent types feature in these representations: high-sided, pitched roofed tents used by the key characters and low slung pitched roofed tents occupied by the rank and file. These seem to be very close in design to the aforementioned earlier Roman tents and it is this similarity combined with a reference in the 600A.D. war poem *Y Gododdin* that prompted *Britannia* to purchase just such an early Roman style tent. The cost of authentic handstitched goatskin meant the use of a dyed fabric as a more economically viable alternative but the proportions are much the same and it provides appropriately authentic looking shelter for both people and kit.

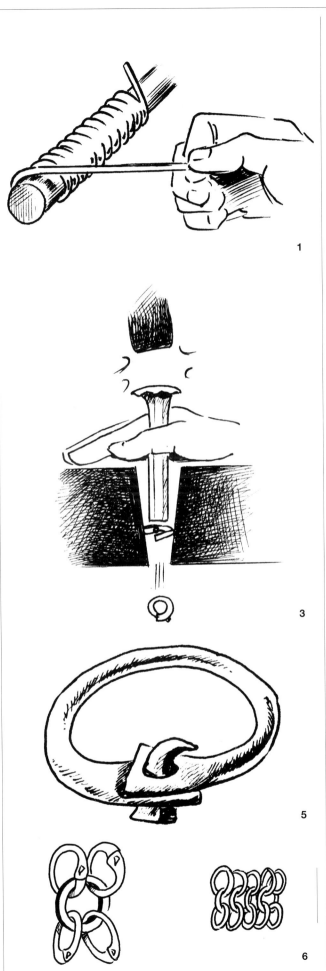
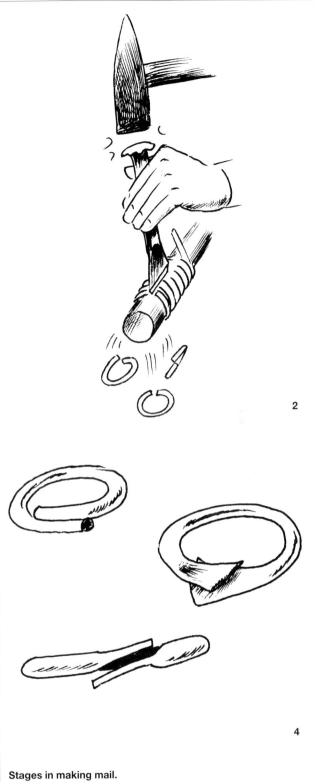

Stages in making mail.

1. The process of ringmail manufacture. Wire is wound around a metal bar.
2. This produces a coil which is then chopped off the bar to produce links.
3. Links are then forced into a tapering hole until they overlap.
4. This overlap is then hammered flat.
5. A small chip of metal is then inserted and hammered like a rivet.
6. The basic pattern of mail is a 1-through-4 combination.

Late Roman heavy infantry/cavalryman wearing a cuirass of lamellar. Reconstruction by Dan Shadrake. Matt Shadrake.

The Warrior

Look at specific war gear even as far back as the 3rd century A.D. and one thing becomes clear – the Roman army like any of its modern counterparts was eclectic in its mix of equipment, although the parade ground tells a different story to life on campaign. Listening to a veteran of the second World War recently, who was involved in the Normandy landings and the push into Europe, he painted a picture of Allied soldiers wearing enemy and even civilian coats and boots for warmth. Throughout the centuries soldiers have adapted their kit for comfort and ease of use. This must have been equally true of the Roman army especially in the later centuries, when a less standardised army with perhaps only a device on a shield would serve to define its numbers as Roman. This would certainly be the case following the Roman policy of accepting foreign troops or *Foederati* into the army to defend parts of the weakening empire; Britain was no exception and it is a long held belief that this policy of using foreign troops to shore up the crumbling borders opened the floodgates for the barbarian peoples to sweep away what was left of Roman society.

Post Roman war gear would be subject to many new demands, in particular that of monetary constraints which dictated to a large degree the change from the earlier Roman style of well trained infantrymen fighting in heavy armour with large convex rectangular shields using thrusting movements with their short swords – all of which meant that armies were now too expensive to equip, train and maintain and hence became obsolete at least a century before the collapse of the western Roman administration. The decline in discipline as well as new political and military pressures were to take their toll on the army as an effective fighting force, as the later Roman writer Vegetius records when he laments the neglect of training and advocates a return to the tougher, more stringent standards of the earlier years, his actual words being: 'Negligence and sloth having by degrees introduced a total relaxation of discipline, the soldiers began to consider their armour too heavy and seldom put it on. They first requested leave from the emperor to lay aside the cuirass and afterwards the helmet.'

Procopius offers a slightly different view when writing about the *Arborychi* (a Christian *foederati* force

Reverse (inside) of the lamellar suit, note the large amount of lacing used. Matt Shadrake.

loyal to Rome) of northern Gaul: 'For even at the present day they are clearly recognised as belonging to the legions to which they were assigned in ancient times, and they always carry their own standards when they enter battle, and always follow the customs of their fathers. And they preserve the dress of the Romans in every particular, even as regards their shoes.'

What was true of northern Gaul can be safely assumed to have been doubly so in a more conservative Britain where the *mores* and even the Latin tongue of the Romans survived in purer form than across the Channel, and for far longer. Notwithstanding differences in strength and appearance from region to region, the Roman infantry would never again be as effective and as standardised as it was in the 1st-2nd centuries A.D., and by the 4th century the emphasis shifted to cavalry, a development of great significance in the evolution of Romano-British warfare.

Helmets
To preserve the safety of its participants, *Britannia* has made a point of studying what can pass for suitable protective headgear for the time period in question.

Early Saxon loom. Pat and Nick Nethercoat.

The easily recognised early Roman Imperial Gallic helmets seem to have been replaced in the 3rd century by both the *spangenhelm* (a conical or dome helmet made up of segments riveted together by a framework of iron bands) and the Sassanid (Persian) style 'Ridge' helmet.

The 'Ridge' helmet seems to have been introduced as a more economical alternative to the Imperial Gallic and the frequency of finds of this particular item throughout Europe, coupled with a recent quote for the manufacture of each from a reproduction armourer, left us in no doubt that these latter helmets were very common, produced without exceptional cost and endured the test of years; in some cases, surviving (with adaptations or merely as a heavy influence) for centuries! There seem to be two main categories of 'Ridge' helmet, the heavy and light versions; the common features of both are the two half bowl sections joined together by means of a slightly raised band or ridge, this is riveted to both halves and cheek and neck guards are suspended from the main dome by means of leather straps, giving ease of movement and flexiblity of fitting – one bowl might change heads several times in its lifetime, with the cheek and neck

Woad plant, used by dyers to obtain greens, blues and in some cases black. Pat Nethercoat.

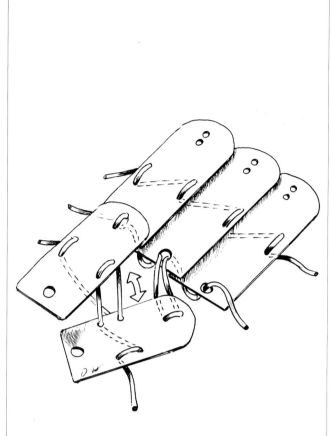

Construction of lamellar. Dan Shadrake.

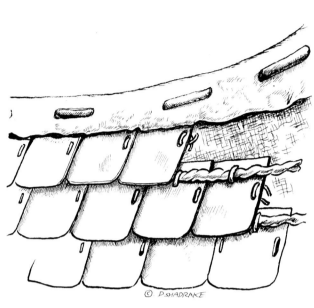

Scales found at Carpow Perthshire. Dan Shadrake.

guards adapted to suit the wearer. The 'light' infantry/cavalry version as it is called, is little more than what has just been described and it is this permutation that occurs in greater frequency, some examples having been found in Germany (Worms), Hungary (Intercisa), and Switzerland (Augst). It is thought that the punched holes were to take a leather edge; this innovation would save even further on production costs as a ragged unfinished edge could be hidden behind rawhide with very little time or skill. The parallels we seek with continental evidence for the persistence of Roman equipment are perhaps best illustrated by the heavy 'Ridge' helmet; moreover, a British example was found in Burgh Castle on the East Anglian coast whose counterparts in the former Yugoslavia (Berkasovo) and Hungary (Concesti) are strikingly similar. The Burgh castle helmet was composed of four segmented iron plates 1.5mm thick that were fixed together with a crest and two reinforcing side bands (32mm wide where they meet the crest, 75mm wide at the rim). Copper alloy rivets (3mm diameter shanks, 4mm diameter heads) were used in its construction and the crest itself was made from a ridge of folded iron (standing 15mm high and

running from the front to the back of the helmet) not the hollow semi-tubular crest present on its Berkasova counterpart and Vendel descendants (see Viking chapter). This crest was folded out at the bottom to produce flanges (8-10 mm wide)which would be riveted to the plates that make up the helmet bowl. The helmet was found in a very dilapidated state and it was only by comparisons with continental examples that any sort of reconstruction was originally attempted. Although elements of the cheek guards and brow band survive it is quite impossible to reach any conclusions on the overall appearance of the original and so this helmet has been subject to a wide variety of interesting interpretations by several reconstruction artists and re-enactment armourers. Despite its poor condition the Burgh castle helmet is one of the few examples of this style where the structure can be so closely examined, as the surviving continental examples are in most cases represented only by the 'husk' or skin of precious metal (the structure of the iron dome has often long since perished).

The two or four piece segments, joined by a raised band running from the front to the back of the helmet, and the one piece 'T'- shaped nose-guard/eyebrow piece riveted to a band running around the lower rim of the dome, both conform to a curve above either eye which adds to the aesthetic appeal and increases the wearer's field of vision, although this is slightly more visually restrictive than the light 'Ridge' helmet; the larger, heavier cheek and neck guards are obviously designed to take a greater deal of punishment indicating that these were perfect helmets for fighting in heavy and close formation. As re-enactors with more than a few dents in our reconstructed helms, we say this with confidence.

The basic 'Ridge' helmet design does not alter. Even though individual finds are separated by distances of hundreds of miles, it is therefore a reasonable assumption that what is found in Europe can be accepted in Britain, provided it can be shown that a similar military need for it would apply. This philosophy can be applied more easily during the last years of Roman rule but gets harder to justify the further we go into the Dark Ages. Sadly no British examples of *spangenhelms* survive. Although this is not an argument against their existence in Britain. The *spangenhelm* as opposed to the 'Ridge' Helmet is one where the construction of the dome uses segments rather than one piece or two piece bowls, and is found throughout Europe. Egypt and Holland have both yielded excellent examples of *spangenhelms* from whose remains have been ascertained the following details – the Egyptian example (Der el Medineh) was made up of six plates riveted to six bands capped by a disc, again riveted at the top and with a ring attached to the disc whose function may have been decorative or practical, for either the fixture of crests or plumes or for carrying purposes. Around the rim of this Egyptian helm a brow band was riveted, this arched over each eye and included a nasal piece of T-shape. In this latter aspect it was similar to the 'Ridge' Helmet. Cheek pieces and neck guard were attached to the helm by means of hinges. The example from Holland (Rijksmuseum van Oudheden, Leiden) is similar but has only four plates and four bands. Examples of *spangenhelm* are represented as early as the second century A.D., as the Syrian archers on Trajan's column appear to be wearing them. The *spangenhelm*-type construction re-occurs throughout the Dark Ages across most European and Middle Eastern military cultures, which neatly returns us to our argument for their existence in Britain.

No reference exists to tell us how helmets were

Representation of lamellar on the 'Isola Rizza' dish, note the downward facing radial pattern of scales. Dan Shadrake.

Fragment of tunic from *Vindolana*. Dan Shadrake.

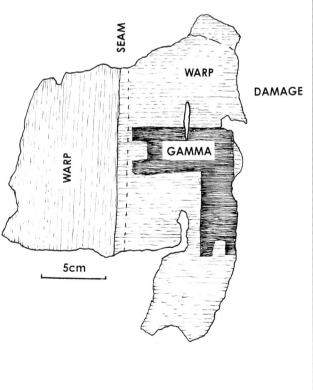

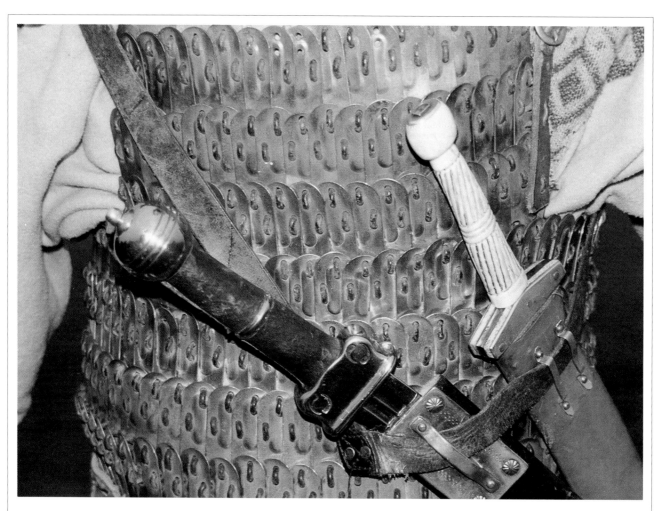

Spatha and side-arm. *Spatha* reconstructed by *Armourclass*. The spatha cross-guard is based on the 4th century example from Nydham bog. The side-arm has an earlier *Pugio* blade (based on 3rd century examples found in the Thames) and the bone handle is based on the example from Buch.

padded, but several experiments with quilted leather and sheepskin (fixed and detachable) linings have produced some effective results. Another form of headgear is the pillbox hat or the 'Pannonian cap.' Vegetius recommends the wearing of this item to make men accustomed to wearing helmets – no archaeological examples survive but there is no shortage of good evidence on sculptural and pictorial references throughout the later Roman Empire. Following their initial introduction, in fur, leather and fabric into *Britannia's* re-enactment circles they were met with some derision, but now they are worn by most of the society and we even get requests from the public to sell our 'Pannonians', especially on cold days.

Shields

The principal form of protection and unit identification was the shield, and yet this is the most commonly overlooked aspect of kit in terms of construction and design. By the 4th century the bronze edged, square sided *scutum* had long since dropped out of service and the changing tactics, new enemies and a crippled economy meant that, as with helmets and indeed all items of military equipment, cheaper, easier alternatives had to be found. The shields of the later empire were either convex or flat in profile an either round or oval in shape. The ovals are the most commonly represented in pictorial evidence and archaeological finds of the late Roman era. By far the best archaeological evidence was found at Dura Europos in Syria. A total of 24 shield boards was found in varying conditions of preservation. The most complete examples were obtuse ovals and were an average of 3 foot wide by 4 foot high. These were slightly convex and were made of poplar planks that had been glued together. The remains of earlier-style rectangular, curved shields were also found at Dura Europos. These were constructed using a form of plywood. This consisted of three layers of wood running alternately horizontally and vertically. These had been glued together to form the shield body and were covered in hide and linen. Shield reconstructions of the late Roman era tend to use modern plywood and are covered in fabric or leather. Most reconstructions are intended for use on the battle re-enactment field and therefore the time and energy devoted to faithful methods of shield reproduction would be wasted on shield woods which have an average life of one to three seasons.

One person who has specialised in the faithful reproduction of the Dura Europos shields is Jeff Brimble of the *VIIIth Augusta* (a Welsh-based re-enactment group concentrating on the early Roman era). His earliest reconstructions included the Dura Europos oval shields. During tests he found the convex ovals to be more effective as they were more difficult to pull away from the body in combat. With the assistance of the Roman Research Trust he was also able to reconstruct the earlier style rectangular shields (62 cm x 93 cm, thickness 1.8 cm). The total weight without reconstructed shield boss was 3.6 kgs. This was based on fragment B (discovered by Franz Cummont in 1926). This reconstruction took 40 hours to make and through experimentation he was able to refute the theory that shields were toughened by a baking process, and the suggestion that the original shields were made using large presses and stone formers also seemed unlikely to him in view of the difficulties posed by the variability of the behaviour of the wood components under pressure.

He suggests that each layer (consisting of strips of wood) may have been constructed separately inside a large steam room or bathhouse and when one considers the frequency of bathhouses within the empire this seems plausible. He used local timber in his reconstruction (oak, birch and plane) and cut straight and knot-free pieces from wood in its green state and boiled the wood rather than steamed it. He glued the alternate layers together; not having access to the original bull-hide glue, he used a modern replacement that had the same degree of flexibility. He also used a sheet of hessian between each layer as a shock absorber and to assist the adhesion. These complicated methods of construction were well within the capabilities of the earlier Roman military society, and it is an inviting thought that perhaps the famous *scutum* with its large curved surface fell out of favour because of a deterioration in the type of facilities needed to produce them. This would tie in with the adoption by the (much) later military machine of cheaper materials and methods for equipping the army.

In *Britannia* we have found that the addition of a thin piece of hessian to the face of a shield before

Replica of the Koln *spatha*, using wood as a substitute for ivory. Replica by Armourclass.

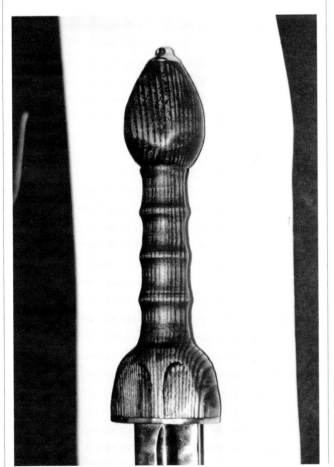

Late Roman infantrymen wearing tunics that have applied patterns of solid colour. Derek Clow.

painting can vastly increase its lifespan, soaking up blows and holding the wood together once it becomes unstable from constant use. Here, as in the area of shield decoration, *Britannia* has evolved a radical approach to authenticating kit by practical application.

The subject of pigments for shield decoration is open to speculation; *Britannia's* approach has been to collect information from several key sources, namely pigment specialists from the Royal Asiatic Society (appropriate in view of the Romans' own sources for many of their more exotic dyestuffs), art restorers and of course the British Museum. Reviewing all of this information, we formed the conclusion that pigments were directly applied to the fabric covering the shield front in what we would suggest was a 'fresco' technique (applying paint directly on to wet plaster, nothing more than wet ground up chalk, for a more vivid image) as the 6th century poem *Y Gododdin* describes in its reference to a 'chalked' shield. If indeed the late/post Roman chose to apply earth or vegetable colours to a wet ground-chalk surface, the effect would have been quite striking as the colours would have been more vibrant and more intense.

Quite a good range of colours would have been available to the shield painter, even with the lack of

Sword detail from the Tetrarch sculpture in Venice.

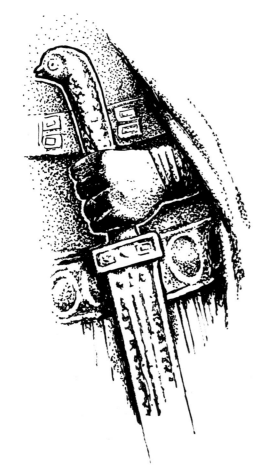

trade and an unstable economy; reds, browns and yellows from earth pigments, greens and blues from vegetable dyes like woad (from the *isatis tinctoria* plant), blacks from burning charcoal or bones without air. By far the best source for late Roman shield designs is the aforementioned *Notitia Dignitatum*. Although what survives of this important Roman document of Empire-wide troop and equipment dispositions are only a couple of mediaeval facsimiles (one at Oxford, one at Munich), it is sufficiently reliable to be used as a guide to shield patterns extant in the 4th century and, by projection, beyond into the Dark Ages. Serious re-enactors of the 5th century are adopting various designs from the many to choose from in this source, and *Britannia* in its later Roman incarnation selected the shield motif of the *Secunda Britanniarum*, because part of that unit was listed as deployed on the Saxon Shore (*Britannia's* home territory) and because the shield design itself has much to recommend it, being both bright, easily recognised at a distance and simple to paint and repair. Its radial red spoke pattern on a yellow oval has become a signature for the group.

The bronze edging had long been replaced by

The average re-enactment spear is between 6-7ft long. Mike Brown, English Heritage.

Detail from the Roman tomb (name unknown) in Gamizgrad, former Yugoslavia. The horseman appears to be carrying an axe. His clothing shows that he is unlikely to be a landworker and therefore the axe is more likely to be a weapon or mark of office than a utilitarian tool. The infantryman is wearing what appears to be a ridge helmet and carrying a long broad-headed spear. Nick Nethercoat.

rawhide, for reasons of cost; this is simulated by modern re-enactors who choose to edge their shields with rawhide dog chews – as comical as this sounds it greatly prolongs the shield's field life, in some cases for years. Despite the surviving 3rd century examples from Dura Europos (which are thought far too intricately painted to be for regular military use) little or nothing survives except for the shield boss, and in most cases British finds of this era are identified as Saxon. Whether this shows that the Romano-British forces were conquered outright and left little or nothing of their military technology (unlikely when examining other aspects of evidence) or whether the predominantly Christian Britons were therefore not likely to commit any goods to the grave, remains a mystery and part of the continuing attraction of this era.

Body Armour

No one would deny that the most difficult area for sub-Roman era re-enactors is that of armour in its reference and reconstruction. Whereas earlier and later centuries have a good ratio of visual reference and archaeological finds, this information is as rare as hens' teeth by the 5th century. Turning to possible historical explanations for this scarcity, we can conjecture that the breakdown of Roman administration and the commercial base which depended upon it (which we would hastily add did not occur overnight but over decades) would have meant that the mass production of metal armour would have wound down, perhaps to the extent that only a few craftsmen would have retained the skill and knowledge to make and repair the scale, lamellar and ring-mail armours which were familiar to soldiers throughout the Empire. This is not to say that these things suddenly ceased to exist, just that they were not produced in large quantities for regular militia, nor was the quality of manufacture consistent as sources of raw materials faltered, dried up and cheaper or more convenient alternatives were adopted. One of the theories which has been tested and gained ground accordingly is that, in the absence of *fabricae* churning out ring-mail links or scale armour, abundant natural protective materials such as

Recreated late 5th century A.D. Arthurian Britons. The figure on the left is wearing a boiled leather cuirass *(Britannia).* G. Lee.

The spear was a common weapon amongst the rank and file.

leather or horn would have been pressed into service. This is not to say that petty kings, warlords, chieftains and those lucky enough to inherit did not have these more archaic armours, only that they were not produced for mass distribution on the grand scale of their Roman predecessors.

The Great Leather Debate

The 'muscled' leather cuirass is dismissed by many researchers as artistic preference for classical convention; this view is reinforced by the abundance of sculptural, numismatic and other clear visual references although there is little in the way of actual archaeological material to support it. From this we may suppose that either it did not exist as an actual military item or was so rarely produced that it was for parade rather than campaign use. *Britannia* and several other research/re-enactment groups have experimented with leather hide armour with some surprising results; when boiled, moulded to the shape required and then left to dry, thick hide becomes almost as hard as mild steel. In its changed form,

leather thus treated can resist impact as effectively as most metal armours and is almost as impervious to sharp blade thrusts; indeed in the authors' experience leather can often absorb and disperse impact energy more efficiently due to its composition. This leather hardening process is often called 'cuir-bouilli'. Unfortunately, the British climate has left us with no examples of leather hide body armour, but here again, casting the net wider, we have considered that the two thigh defences of rawhide lamellar which were found at Dura Europos in Syria are indicative of the readiness of provincial military establishments to adopt leather hide as a practical alternative to bronze or iron. This leather 'scale' armour find has lifted leather hide armour out of the realms of fantasy and has prompted several members of *Britannia* to reconstruct body armour using the Dura Europos finds as a credible foundation. *Britannia* has kept its leather armour to a minimum, not just because of controversy but for the practical reasons that follow: leather hide armour has the advantage of being durable, lightweight and relatively corrosion free but its major disadvantage is that exposure to the more British elements of excessive rain, sleet snow and mist for any length of time or merely immersion in water (whilst fording a wide river, for instance) would greatly reduce its protective value by causing it to become waterlogged and thus too flexible; in fact Pliny the Elder refers to hippopotamus skin armour and states that it was 'useless when wet'. It is important to realise that leather hide armour, as opposed to the soft leather 'armour' used on stage and screen, is also quite inflexible and therefore best used for torso or upper arm/leg defences, and of course, horse armour. This latter category has received a notable boost with the finds of leather fragments of chamfrons from the Hadrian's Wall forts of Newstead and Vindolanda. Peter Connolly has reconstructed such a chamfron using the leather remains as a pattern; the result is a useful reminder that leather most certainly was valued for its protective qualities by the Romans, and it would be absurd to imagine that Arthurian Britons would disregard it. After all, leather was one commodity that would not have been in short supply as rural life continued among the *pagani* of Britain.

Ringmail

Ringmail is a flexible protective surface made from interlocking iron wire links and its versatility has ensured its longevity in a military application from around the 4th century B.C. to the 1st World War (in fact its protective and flexible properties are still recognized by modern industry). Its invention is often credited to the Celts, in fact the Roman writer Varro refers to this type of armour as 'Gallic'. Ringmail is more resistant to edged weapons than to crushing blows; for this reason a padded garment was worn underneath the mail, and sometimes leather *pteruges* (protective and decorative straps) would hang from this. Examples of Roman ringmail have been found in Caerleon, and the remains of a knee and elbow-length suit was found at Vimose. In earlier representations (such as the representation on the tombstone in Colchester of

The *Gaesum*, found at Carvoran, Northern Britain.

Centurion Marcus Favonius Facilis) a type of shoulder doubling was employed but in many later depictions such as the 4th century 'Biblical' soldier wearing wrist and thigh length mail (Via Latina Catacomb, Rome) this element is distinctly absent. The construction of mail even for a modern re-enactor is laborious and time consuming, even with the advantages of modern tools and materials; instead, many understandably opt for square section spring-washers (6-8mm) in a dark metallic finish. This is frowned upon by many living history purists who prefer to use only round section wire for their links, but in the defence of those who opt for the washers, there are examples of stamped square section mail used alternately with round section wire as strong reference; a good example is the fragment from Carlingwalk Loch. The problems facing the re-enactor are mostly those of time, cost and the need to carry out quick repairs and with this in mind, spring washers offer a practical and relatively cheap solution as well as looking reasonably authentic. The costume makers and armourers in several recent films have enhanced the productions by using this method of mail manufacture instead of the usual knitted and silver sprayed string, which of course doesn't hang right, having no weight behind it, and always gets a laugh when it flaps up in the wind! The ancient method of mail manufacture however, was complex and time consuming; firstly wire was drawn to a standard thickness, then wound around a narrow bar, then this coil was chopped off the bar resulting in tiny open links of metal. These links were then forced through a narrowing hole causing the link ends to overlap; these ends were hammered flat and pierced so that a small wedge of metal could be inserted which would act as a rivet, sealing the link closed. The basic pattern of mail is a four-through-one formation and once a few links are joined the familliar mail pattern begins to emerge. It was used mainly as body armour but its flexibility and durability meant that it had other applications as well (on the aventail of the later 7th century Coppergate helmet, for instance). An

The *Gaesum* in use. John Eagle.

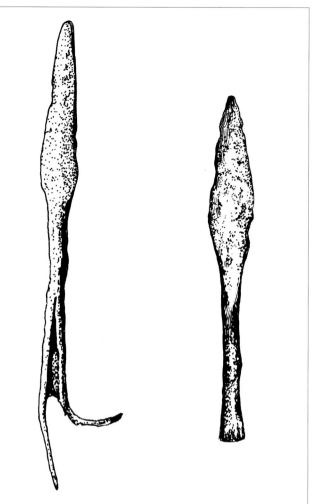

(Left) Catterick spear. (Right) Roman spearhead, Caerleon.

interesting image of third century soldiers wearing what appears to be mail coifs is depicted in the 'Battle of Ebenezer' fresco (Synagogue at Dura) and images in the *Vergilius Vaticanus* manuscript (4th century) show a group of soldiers wearing what appears to be mail or scale coifs in conjunction with elbow length mail shirts. The representations of scale and mail are rather confused, as the ancient artists, sculptors and jewellers tended to use a variety of techniques for these textures, including zig-zags, herringbone, dots or just crude lines. So vague are the appropriate visual clues that until a reliable archaeological example comes to light, many late Roman and early Dark Age groups will obviously be reluctant to attempt reconstructions, if only to avoid tiresome arguments about anachronisms. The use of mail undoubtedly continued in Britain through the 4th-6th centuries and beyond, and following the collapse of the large scale military manufacturing system its value meant that it would have been worn mainly by the military elite; of course it would not have been provided for the common soldier unlike in the earlier centuries. In the 6th century poem *Y Gododdin* the poet Aneirin describes an elite force of cavalry: 'Spear-shafts held

aloft with sharp points, And shining mail-shirts and swords.'

Britannia, like many other Roman, Dark Age and mediaeval societies has a good selection of mailshirts and the problems of manufacture, repair and rust removal are common to all; in addition, the consequence of the weight of the mail, even with comparatively fine examples, has meant that many re-enactors who specialise in this era have sought alternative methods of body armour.

Scale Armour

Unlike ring mail, scale armour is easy to produce and lighter but less flexible and not as protective, there are hundreds of diverse surviving examples from the Roman era, mostly in bronze, although occasionally they are tinned or gilded such as the example found in Chester. The scales occur in a variety of shapes and sizes but were thought to have been almost always backed with fabric; this is supported by a few examples which actually bear traces of fabric on the reverse. For all its advantages, this type of armour is vulnerable to upward thrusts as a sword or spear point can easily be forced underneath the scales to penetrate the fabric backing. By far the best find to illustrate the structure and backing of scale is the example found in a pit at the legionary base at Carpow in Perthshire during 1979 excavations; a handful of small bronze scales (around 1cm across) were discovered, still fixed to their linen backing, with the scales joined to each other horizontally by means of wire links, which were loosely passed through holes in the side of each scale. Each complete row of scales was then placed on the fabric backing, a strand of yarn was passed over each set of upper holes, and the thread that attached the scales to the backing sheet was passed through one of the upper holes over the yarn and back through the remaining upper hole. The process was repeated on the next row, the armourer/soldier taking care to overlap the yarn fixing on the row below. Many modern re-enactors have decided to reproduce scale armour quite faithfully, but a few choose instead to rivet modern mild steel scales directly onto soft leather, because even at close scrutiny the impression is equally convincing. Here again, the advantage of total accuracy set against time, cost and ease of repair has to be carefully weighed up. Heavy infantry reconstructions of the period can certainly look impressive and tie in well with the 4th century writer Ammianus' reference to 'gleaming' armour. Again, Aneirin the poet, talking in the 6th century, refers to 'dark blue armour' in *Y Gododdin*, by which we think he meant not painted armour, but the deep blue sky reflected off well maintained cavalry armour. The practice of gilding and silvering was certainly used throughout the Roman era and beyond; this involved beating out gold or silver into a thin foil and covering an object such as armour scale using a solder. Tinning was a much simpler process in which the armour components would be dipped in molten tin which, as this has a lower melting point than bronze, would coat the object in tin. It is worth mentioning that armourer Ivor Lawton of *Dawn of Time Crafts* recently experimented with tinned bronze; the result was a very impressive 'silver-like' coating on some belt plates and it is easy to see why the Romans and subsequent peoples selected this rather flamboyant finish for their armour.

Lamellar

Even as late as the third and 4th centuries the Roman empire was a great melting-pot of cultures and ideas. Military technology was no exception, and in fact the longevity of the Roman war machine is often attributed to its chameleon-like ability to absorb and improve upon the more successful inventions and innovations borrowed from people within its borders

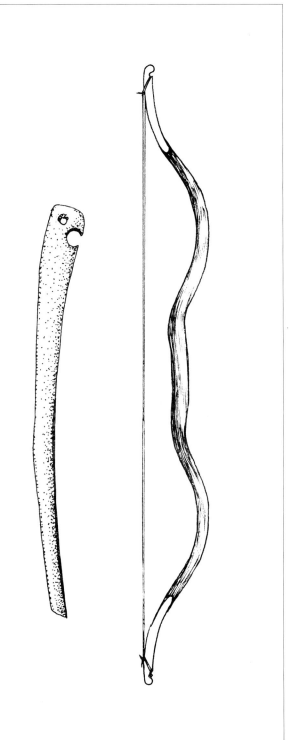

(Left) Barr Hill ear laths made of antler (from a composite bow). (Right) Composite bow.

and beyond. The end result of this cross-cultural information exchange was to introduce weapons and armour to far flung peoples, who might otherwise have never encountered such a diversity of military technology. The introduction of an unusual eastern scale armour (referred to as lamellar) into western Europe and Britain in the late 3rd century A.D. is an excellent illustration of this point; lamellar consisted of long narrow scales laced both horizontally and

Lamellar armour is surprisingly flexible and protective and because of its construction it is not vulnerable to upward thrusts.

vertically to its neighbours and because of its self contained lacing construction it needed no leather backing.

Modern reconstructions have scales of hide, bronze or mild steel, and are comparatively easily produced by expert and inexpert alike; maintenance and repair are similarly straightforward. Lamellar provides a surprisingly flexible and protective surface, as blows against a single scale are absorbed by its eight surrounding neighbours. Several examples have been found in Britain; two small round-ended examples were found at Corbridge but perhaps the most valuable and interesting find is the relatively large mass of iron lamellar plates found in Somerset. These have rusted into a dilapidated cluster, in which the average size of these scales is around 2.8cm wide x 5cm high; more importantly, the structure of the actual leather lacing has been preserved in what amounts to a positive cast by the action of the sulphides produced by the corrosion of the surrounding metal scales. The leaching of the sulphides into the organic material, in this case leather,

has gradually replaced the original fibres whilst retaining their form. Despite its poor condition, this find provides excellent insight into the construction of lamellar and (perhaps more valuable to *Britannia* and associated re-enactment societies) conclusive proof that it was actually used in Britain. There are a variety of lamellar plates and more than one method of lacing, although the Romano-British finds so far suggest the most basic method of construction which is what *Britannia* has so far chosen to emulate. Designs for complete suits of lamellar have so far been drawn from slightly later depictions in Byzantine ikons and numismatic examples in the absence of contemporaneous reference. One particular lamellar suit reconstruction drew upon the 'Isola Rizza' dish for inspiration, this 6th century Lombardic or Byzantine silver plate has the relief design of a lamellar-clad cavalryman shown in remarkable clarity; of particular interest is the shoulder-guard with its downward facing radial pattern of lamellar plates. This feature was reconstructed without great difficulty although the authors felt the addition of large belts and buckles for quick release (should access be required for first aid) were necessary.

Tunics

The conditions in which ancient textiles survive free from damaging bacterial activity are quite rare, particularly in Britain and most of Northern Europe, the exceptions in this type of climate being peat bogs and deep lakes where constant moisture, consistent temperature and lack of air have, in rare cases, contributed to the preservation of fabrics. The most common materials used in Roman and Dark Age Britain were wool and linen, although fragments of silk from the Roman era (indicating trade with Syria and the far East) have been found in Colchester (Essex) and Holborough (Kent). Aside from Northern Europe, the desert conditions of Egypt have little of the debilitating bacterial activity which destroys fabric and many hundreds of examples of later Roman-style tunics, cloaks and general remnants have survived in an excellent state of preservation. On the other hand, the rather poor and infrequent textile finds of Britain have meant that it is necessary to study what is available outside the geographical confines of these islands to produce a better picture of clothing of the time. The designs incorporated into the Coptic tunics of Roman Egypt aligns well with what we know of

tunics from depictions of clothing on mosaics and frescoes throughout the later Roman empire (San Vitale in Ravenna, Via Latina Catacombs in Rome and closer to home a figure on the mosaic floor of a 4th century villa at Brantingham). The authors have been fortunate enough to purchase a fragment of an early 6th century linen tunic for study and replication. The fragment was situated on the shoulder area of the tunic and was actually woven into the fabric (obviously the cost of reproducing this process faithfully is currently beyond the means of the average re-enactment society). It must also be borne in mind that the context of this Coptic cloth may not necessarily have been a military one, although the Coptic style of tunic is encountered throughout the later Roman empire particularly in military settings (the Vindolanda fragment). For the purposes of re-enactment we are currently investigating the possibility of silk-screening a facsimile of this original design directly on to linen tunics, but for the immediate future we have decided to reproduce the decorations in solid colour sewn onto an off-whitewool or linen garment. There are several examples of these coloured ornamental decorations being sewn on rather than forming part of the weave, although some are tacked on in a very crude fashion, possibly indicating that they were cut from an earlier badly damaged tunic and considered too precious to

Reconstructed Roman boot by Ivor and Simone Lawton, *Dawn of Time Crafts*.

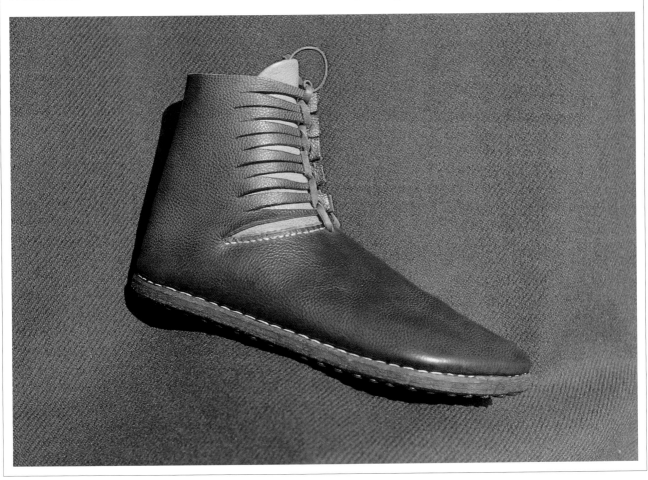

Late 3rd Century Roman boot from Germany. Iain Bell

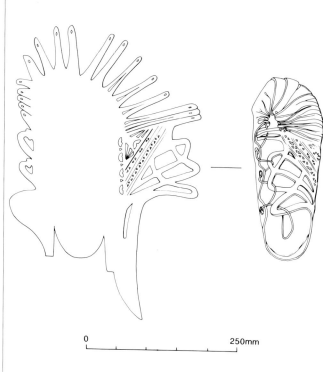

Saalburg boot. Iain Bell (after Hahne 1915-20).

simply discard, all of which is very encouraging to amateur tunic makers in late Roman re-enactment since a high quality finish is not a pre-requisite for once! The Coptic tunics were thought to be woven complete on looms that were wide enough to take the entire length of the tunic, back and front, leaving a slit for the neck. When finished the tunic was simply sewn up the sides to give the impression of a seamless garment. The day has yet to arrive when such a loom is up and running for re-enactment purposes. There were few major developments in textile manufacture and dyeing processes in the last half of the first millenium; most re-enactment societies concentrating on representing northern European armies tend to use wool or linen for clothing. Fragmentary examples of these materials are present in many European Dark Age grave finds as well as strong evidence for continued importation of Chinese or Indian silks even after the collapse of the western Roman Empire. Vegetable fibres such as cotton are largely absent as the bacteria present on corpses tends to turn its attention towards this material very rapidly (as any modern police pathologist will attest). Cotton fibres at ancient sites have been dismissed in many cases as

modern 'contamination' during the course of excavations. Late Roman and Dark Age societies tend to use wrist and knee-length wool tunics. These are dyed with a variety of natural materials including: onion skins (yellow or brown), madder root (red), oak tannin or walnut husks (dark brown), dyer's greenweed or flowerheads of reeds (green), elder bark and meadowsweet (black, although opinion differs on the ability of obtaining colour-fast blacks), and the woad plant (blues or greens). Woad plants have been grown by Pat Nethercoat of *Britannia's* living history section; this broad leafed plant was used to dye wool in a variety of greens and blues. The subject of textiles and dyeing processes has been explored by specialists both in and out of historical recreation, including Russell Scott (N.F.P.S.) Ben Levick *(Regia Anglorum)* and first and foremost Jill Goodwin, one of the country's leading exponents of natural dyeing, whose books, articles and letters have been a constant source of enlightenment and helpfulness and without whom the ancient craft of textile dyeing would have lost so much of its traditional knowledge.

Garments of re-enactors are usually edged or decorated in one of two ways, either with hand embroidery or with tablet woven braids. Tablet weaving is believed to have started about 3,000 years ago and was chiefly known in China, Japan, North Africa and also Europe, so we can safely use it in the knowledge that it has remained relevant throughout recorded history. The best known tablet weaving find has been that of the Osberg ship burial of 850A.D. where 52 tablets were discovered. Tablets were commonly made of wood, bone, or leather, whichever was to hand. A great variety of patterns could be obtained by the rotation of the threaded tablets in designated sequences, and this is one area where a small element of luxury and sophistication can be authentically represented whatever the chosen time period.

It is fortunate for the late and post Roman re-enactor that there is plenty of reliable and detailed northern European sources in respect of weaponry in general for this era. In our experience the main problem facing anyone attempting the reconstruction of 4th to 6th century weaponry is one of cultural identification rather than chronological justification. Very few weapons of this era can be said to be Romano-British; this is thought to be due to the influence of Christianity, for simpler burial rituals and disapproval of previous pagan practices meant that personal belongings, including weapons and armour, were no longer interred with the dead but available to a succession of warriors and therefore subject to the necessity of repair and recycling. This theory may explain why most surviving military artifacts of this era are identified as pagan Germanic, particularly in the south of Britain. This is not to say however that every single Romano-Briton, whether town or country dweller, was a Christian, but the influence of Christianity on religious practices in Britain at this time is an historic reality, established on the back of centuries of Roman administration, customs and culture, yet amazingly managing to hang on after the majority of Roman elements were dissolved in the melting pot of the 5th century.

Swords

Swords of the 4th to 6th centuries are well-represented in contrast to the finds of earlier and later centuries, although a particular hazard is the aforementioned cultural confusion; so saturated was the later Romano-British military culture with Germanic imports of swords, belt buckles and other Germanic accessories (following the steady influx of

Deurne boot. Iain Bell (after M.C. Bishop 1993).

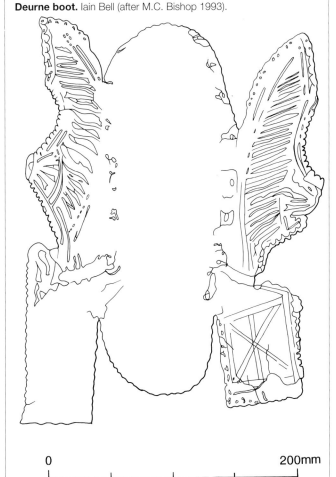

0   200mm

Low Ham boot, a late 3rd/early 4th Century boot. Iain Bell.

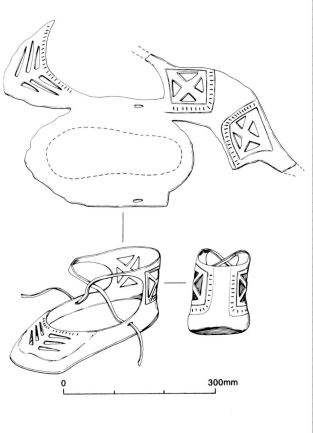

0   300mm

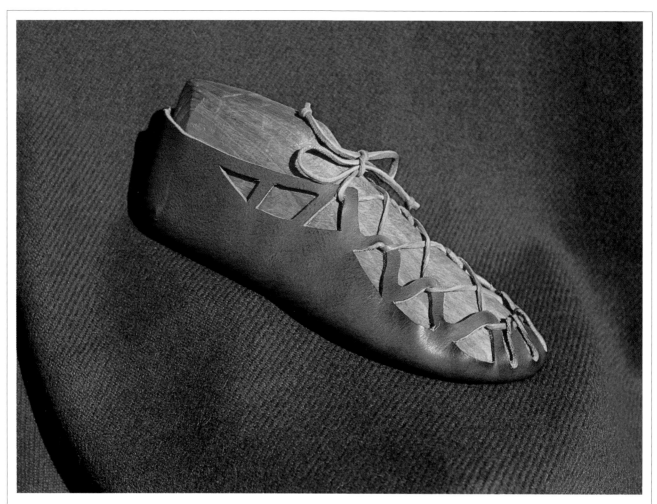

After the 2nd century it was difficult to distinguish military and civil footwear. Reconstruction by Ivor and Simone Lawton, *Dawn of Time Crafts*.

foederati to bolster Britain's defences) that it is now impossible to say whether the bearer of a particular weapon or ornament was Romano-British (whether adhering to a Roman way of life or a more rural/native one), settled Germanic *foederati* (perhaps with Romano-British allegiances) or more recently arrived Saxon, Jute or Angle invader/settler. It is the authors' opinion that re-enactors of this period, particularly after the end of Roman administration, can mix and match the cultural origin of their equipment with ease but in the interests of clarity at public events it sometimes helps to exaggerate the more familiar aspects of these origins – *Britannia's modus operandi* is to standardize the Romano-British ranks (even into the later part of the 5th and early 6th centuries) so as to establish an easily recognised identity contrasting with the undisciplined and indistinct nature of the assorted opposing forces ranged against them. There is no one method of production or common source, let alone template, for the swords of this era; some weapons would have been inherited from earlier generations, some would be in circulation because of the widespread distribution of *foederati* (or foreign mercenaries); at the start of this particular era some would have been imported from the *fabricae* (large scale arms factories) and individual workshops elsewhere in the Roman Empire, whilst some would naturally have been manufactured by craftsmen in this country. So any discussion of individual swords must take these considerations into account, and furthermore one last element which must be added to the equation is the distinct existence of swords of Pictish and Irish provenance – often overlooked, they form a body of work quite outside the normal Romano-British experience due to the geographical isolation from mainstream arms evolution in the Roman world. The members of *Britannia* who represent the Romano-British contingent do, as a general rule, carry swords as a primary weapon, partly because this is a way of showing that they are adopting a quasi-Roman style of equipping an elite fighting force, especially the front ranks; (in this way *Britannia* can straddle the late and post Roman/Arthurian eras with ease) but mainly because swords provide spectacle and excitement at public events, and are the chief means by which conflict can be prolonged for the entertainment (and education, perhaps) of the audience. Spears of course have their place, and we will discuss their role at a later point. Returning to the plethora of sources for swords, we should perhaps say at this point, that by outlining the known types in existence in our chosen era, we are attempting to give a cross section, and a very slim one at that, of the choices open to the re-enactors of these times. As we have already said, bastardization and cross-pollination are just two of the means (battlefield scavenging is yet another) by which the participants of these conflicts would have acquired weapons which were becoming ever scarcer. Turning to our most justifiable source for Romano-British swords in the earlier years of this era, it is important to consider the examples of later Roman *spathae* (long slashing cavalry swords mentioned by Vegetius) which occur throughout Northern Europe, because they are representative of the type of sword which reflected the move away from the more static set piece infantry based battle to the evolving cavalry emphasis which in embryo was the mediaeval style of warfare. When choosing to recreate a late/post Roman *spatha* most Romano-British re-enactors opt for something distinctly Roman in appearance; the example from the 4th century burial at Köln survives intact and provides us with excellent reference both for design and proportions. The parallel blade in this example is 28 inches long by 2 inches wide and has a ribbed ivory grip. Convincing reconstructions have been produced using finds of detached fittings such as the hilt from Butzbach, Germany, in conjunction with the many sculptural representations and archaeological examples. The *spatha* as it was described by the later Roman writer Vegetius was thought to be a Romanised progression of the much earlier Celtic cavalry sword and a helpfully detailed quote from the 2nd century A.D. writer Arrian throws some light on this weapon and its use in cavalry warfare in his military manual the *Ars Tactica*: 'Of the Roman cavalry some carry pikes and charge in the manner of the Alans and Sarmatians and others have lances. They wear a large flat sword suspended from the shoulder and they carry broad oval shields, an iron helmet, an interlocked corset and small greaves. They carry lances both to hurl from far, whenever that is necessary, and to fight off the enemy at close range, and if they have to engage in close combat they fight with their swords'

Sculptural representations of the late Roman sword vary considerably; some have very plain hilts mirrored in actual contemporaneous archaeological finds, and whereas certain examples, such as the stylized eagle hilts featured on the porphyry carving of the Tetrarchs

Later Roman Belt reconstructions by Ivor and Simone Lawton, *Dawn of Time Crafts*.

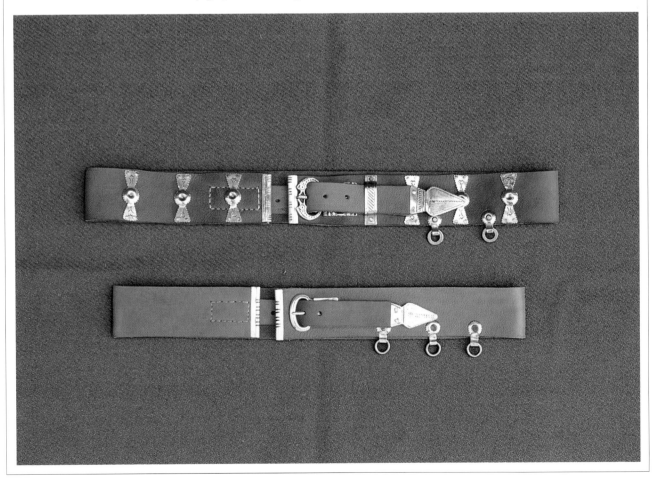

Vienna statue, belt reference. Nick Nethercoat. (after M.C. Bishop 1993).

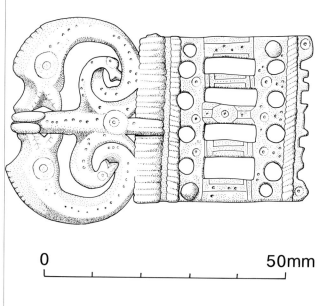

The Colchester buckle. Iain Bell.

0   50mm

have been dismissed as no more than inventions of the sculptor or 'one-offs' commissioned by the imperial hierarchy of the time and therefore of no use in a regular military context, this dismissal is due solely to the absence of actual finds supporting such designs. Therefore we would tentatively venture to suggest that artistic, sculptural and numismatic references, however inviting their straightforward clarity may be, cannot be depended upon to portray the true picture. It is advisable, we feel, to seek parallel evidence to corroborate a reconstruction. Modern armourers have the advantage of consistent quality steel to work on (as opposed to the irregular hand-worked iron of the pre-industrial smithies) and as modern re-enactment blades have to take far more blunt 'blade against blade' punishment than the originals ever had to endure, the materials and techniques used by ancient armourers cannot, and should not always be followed faithfully; the sheer expense of some of these processes (pattern welding for example) is often deterrent enough. What we do know about Roman blade technology tells us that the quality of materials and manufacture can vary enormously from region to

region; J. Lang contrasts examples of higher quality composite blades, where softer iron of a low carbon content is sandwiched between strips of carburised iron (pre-industrial era steel) and poorer quality weaker blades of low carbon iron which do not employ the composite method. The classic side arm of this period is the single-edged war knife, and the *seax*, despite its obvious Saxon connotations, introduced into the Roman Empire (and hence Britain) in the 4th century, is used by both Romano-British and early Germanic groups because it is a handy weapon, inexpensive to produce, easy to maintain, and justifiable because the cultural hybridization which we have already discussed in respect of swords would be equally applicable to this piece of equipment. The single edged knife, used as weapon and tool, lends itself to the interpretation that, by its very universality it was carried by the common soldier and elite warrior alike: 'There did not arm for battle, vigorous with spear and shield, sword and knife, any man who

Opposite.

Surviving copper alloy belt fittings. Buckles (a,b,c, Winchester, d, Catterick). Iain Bell (after M.C. Bishop 1993)

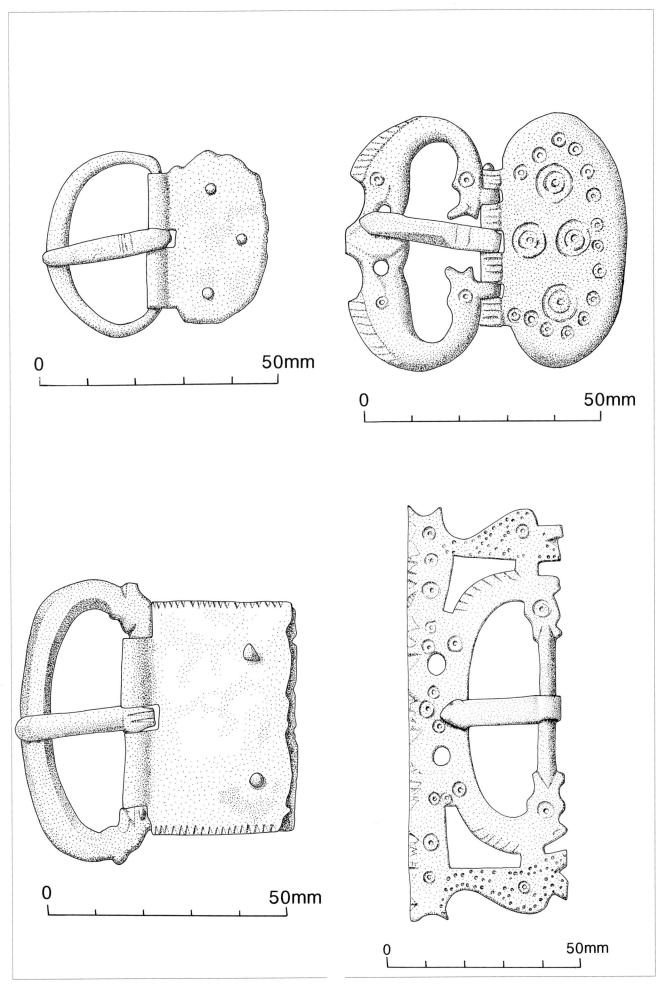

0   50mm

0   50mm

0   50mm

0   50mm

Belt reconstruction by Ben Levick (*Bodgit and Bendit*).

was better...'

This quote, from *Y Gododdin*, illustrates perfectly that knives were to be found on the battlefield wielded by the nobility. Whether one accepts that assertion depends on how much weight is attributed to the information contained within *Y Gododdin*, but that is another investigation in itself.

Axes

Axes are a practical and prolific side arm amongst the Romano-British, Pictish, Irish and Saxon rank and file of this period, smaller and non-descript heads and small hafts are recommended, the bearded and long hafted axe is more suited to the 8th-11th century A.D. Saxon *huscarl*, than the 4th-5th century Saxon invader/settler.

Spears

The spear is the most commonly occurring weapon in this era. As with swords, there are a variety of different types to choose from, sometimes performing different functions. Some are for throwing, some for defence and some merely for training and hunting purposes. These differing functions are determined by weight,

size and style of head. The later Roman writer Vegetius (when referring to the regular army,) describes a variety of shafted weapons; the *lancea* (spear), the *spiculum* (throwing spear, possibly like the Germanic angon)and *plumbatae* (throwing darts). Vegetius refers to throwing darts as *martiobarbuli* and compares them favourably to archers' missiles in their range, and recent tests have been carried out by *Britannia* with variations of these darts allowing for differing lengths of shaft and methods of throwing, both with leather thongs and with under and overarm methods of hand launch. These experiments showed that distances of between 60 and 70 metres were achieved without difficulty by hand launch and greater distances were easily possible using thongs, whether leather or fabric.

Modern re-enactments of Dark Age battles have demonstrated how effective the spear is as a rank and file weapon, as relatively new recruits, with a little elementary training, can hold off the most determined and heavily armoured veterans, providing their formation does not falter or break. It is also worth recognising the spear's limitations and positive drawbacks, as the problems that re-enactors encounter are in many cases identical to those experienced by warriors of the time. In a confined space, such as a melee composed of two opposing sides locked in close conflict, the spear can create more problems than it solves, because lack of space means that more damage can be done to one's own side. The reason for this is that if the spear cannot go forward, then the shaft may be pulled back for a further thrust against the enemy or may be driven back by superior strength, in either case, the result is potential injury from the spear butt, to the unfortunate ranks behind. This is a potential hazard that the re-enactor is well aware of, so too must his ancient counterpart have been.

As for the construction of spears, there are plenty of later Roman or Germanic examples on which a varied range of reconstructions can be based, and a surprisingly high amount of these are from sites in the British Isles. Fairly plain leaf bladed examples from sites such as Catterick and Caerleon provide the basis for a general infantry and cavalry spear; these have fairly long sockets and rounded tips which make for safe and convincing re-enactment spears.

Many Dark Age and mediaeval groups have a minimum thickness and point radius regulation for both swords and spears, which quite sensibly limits the penetrative ability of the reproduction weapon to an

Romano-Briton re-enactors burying a hoard before fleeing the Saxon incursions. Lynne Smith.

almost negligible amount; in many cases, therefore, the reconstructed weapon is subject to a suitable degree of mutation or alteration from an exact facsimile of the original weapon. Due to the skill of many re-enactment armourers these differences are usually so subtly executed that from the spectator's point of view (be they knowledgeable or novice) nothing is amiss. A good example of the need for this adaptation is that which can be applied to the distinct spearhead found at Carvoran in northern Britain. The *gaesum* has a broad and barbed iron head at the end of a long shank; this has echoes of both the earlier Roman *pilum* and the contemporary Germanic *angon* in its appearance but it has been suggested that its function may have been more akin to its Germanic cousin, as both a projectile and a hand held weapon. The heavy head with its sharp point and barbs make it almost too dangerous to reproduce as a re-enactment weapon, not only in its projectile capacity but also in its close order fighting role. Suitable adaptations have been attempted but these come close to caricature in the armourer's compromise for the sake of safety.

The problem of a convincing *spiculum* (throwing spear) for use against personnel at displays has yet to be overcome, as reconstructions using alternative materials with padded heads look neither realistic nor hit the ground with the same dramatic effect as

sharper living history versions. Our compromise has been to demonstrate living history weapons separately to give the public an experience of their effectiveness and accuracy.

The average re-enactment spear length is between 6 and 7ft; this includes the shaft, which is best represented in indigenous hardwoods such as lime, hornbeam (ironwood), ash, or indeed holly; as in *Y Gododdin*: 'Conquerors from their horses' saddles in the van of battle would cast their spears of holly.'

Indigenous hardwoods are certainly more expensive and hard to come by, and therefore cheaper woods can be used, as long as the timber is not liable to shatter and split, which would otherwise create a potential battlefield hazard.

Archery

We have plenty of evidence for the use of the composite bow in Roman Britain. The composite bow was a recurve-style bow with a central shaft of wood that had applied ear-laths of bone (or nocks as they are sometimes known); Barr Hill on the Antonine wall yielded fine examples of antler ear-laths. The range of

Bottom right and left.

Surviving copper alloy belt fittings. Strap ends (from Germany).

Iain Bell (after M.C. Bishop 1993)

such reconstructed bows is greater than that of single piece construction longbows; recent experiments with Persian composite bows have shown them to have had a range of over 350 metres. Arrowhead finds from the later Roman era are widespread throughout the Empire and show a variety of different designs for different applications which are either tanged (Caerleon, Wales) or socketed (Saalburg, Germany).

Slings

We are indebted to a study by W.B. Griffiths *(The Sling and its Place in the Roman Imperial Army)* which explores in depth the full military potential of the slinger. Famous commanders such as Caesar and Xenophon realised the sling's effectiveness and classical writers such as Onasander described its capabilities in some detail: 'The sling is the most deadly weapon that is used by the lightly armed troops, because the lead slug is the same colour as the air and is invisible in its course, so that it falls unexpectedley on the unprotected bodies of the enemy, and not only is the impact itself violent, but also the missile, heated by the friction of this rush through the air, penetrates the flesh very deeply so that it even becomes invisible and the swelling closes over it'.

The damage that could be inflicted by slingers and

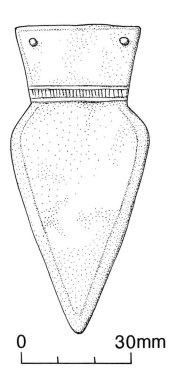

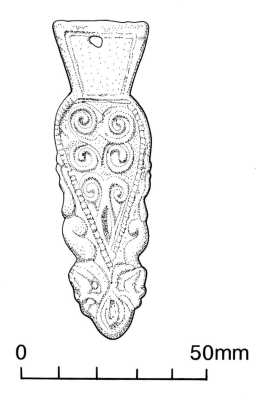

0 ⊢ ⊢ ⊢ ⊢ 30mm

0 ⊢ ⊢ ⊢ ⊢ ⊢ ⊢ 50mm

their missiles was also confirmed by Vegetius who wrote: 'Soldiers...are often more annoyed by the round stones from the sling than by all the arrows of the enemy. Stones kill without mangling the body, and the contusion is mortal without loss of blood'.

Most re-enactors form their shot from soft materials such as mud and clay, which do no damage on impact, apart from a slight loss of dignity.

Xenophon states that Rhodian slingers had twice the range of their Persian counterparts and could outrange the Persian archers. Experiments in range have tended to be conducted by specialist historical researchers such as M. Korfmann (*The Sling as a Weapon*, Scientific American 1973). M. Korfman's experiments showed that the Rhodian sling reconstructions had a range of 230 and 260 metres and their resulting range, which fell a long way short of exceeding the range of the Persian bow, was said by Korfmann to be due to the fact that irregular-shaped natural stones were used as opposed to cast lead, or baked clay shot.

Footwear

Early Roman military boots are characterised by the almost symmetrical shape of their one piece leather upper component which was riveted to an inner leather sole by hobnails. Remains of this style of boot have been found throughout the areas occupied by the Roman army of the first and second centuries and reveal a fairly standardised pattern that did not vary much from region to region. This style of boot seems to have gradually disappeared sometime in the early 2nd century. After this time it is difficult to make distinctions between military and civil footwear; Van Driel Murray suggests that military shoemaking may have passed on to civilians perhaps working on contract and only a proportional imbalance of boot sizes (all adult) may indicate a military community. Military sites from the 2nd century onwards do show an increasing number of women's and indeed children's footwear. A significant number of 3rd century A.D. shoe finds from the Danish and north German bogs reveal trends in Roman footwear and strong parallels in elements such as hobnails and the practice of stamping designs onto the leather uppers. This may indicate strong Roman influence on 3rd century A.D. Germanic fashion, or direct trade with communities outside the Empire at this time. For this reason many people who re-enact the Germanic tribes in the migration era (Saxons, Jutes, and Frisians) tend to use simplified Roman footwear patterns. An interesting development in Roman footwear following the 3rd century is the asymmetrical pattern of the boot uppers such as the Low Ham boot, this seems not only to be a break from traditional Roman bootmaking methods but an interesting link in the evolution of boots towards a more Dark Age pattern. It is also worth mentioning that the practice of hobnailing seems to have ceased in the Western Roman Empire at some time in the 5th century A.D.

Belts

Various styles of military belt and fittings are worn by the members of *Britannia*, and the broader Germanic style belt with its copper alloy mounts and stiffeners, the earlier 3rd century ring buckles (surviving as aged looking re-fits on new leather), and several plainer 'D'-shaped Eastern Roman examples are but a few of the examples chosen for copying.

Most of what we know about later Roman belts (particularly those considered be Germanic) are from burials, and in all but a few cases these are impossible to date specifically due to the lack of significant contemporary equipment sharing the grave sites. In addition the geographic locations of these and other military grave artifacts are not necessarily an indicator of how widespread they really were as the incidence of burial customs of one kind is not a reliable reflection of the total area in which they were worn. Carefully excavated burials obviously provide better insight into the construction of these belts than random finds. Despite the very poor state of most early burials, the belts, if present at all, are very rarely worn by the corpses; in fact most have been placed carefully at the feet of the dead, giving us a better idea of the relative positioning of the buckles, studs, general fittings and sometimes even the dimensions of the leather itself. The Dorchester belt is perhaps the best surviving early Germanic belt found in Britain. Sculptural reference such as the statue of a late Roman Soldier from Vienna is often a good indicator of how late Empire belts were fastened.

A fairly common buckle design of the period is the square fretwork bronze plate with a hinged buckle, often composed of two converging serpent or dolphin heads. The Colchester example is perhaps the finest piece in this category and has been reconstructed for use in *Britannia*. When mounted on a plain leather belt with contemporary (Richborough) 'propeller' stiffeners, this provides a convincing demonstration of how it is possible to take components from different sources but with a common cultural background and make them work together, surely just as the warriors of Arthurian Britain would have had done, whether out of necessity or Celtic creativity. This is the ethos of *Britannia* and indeed most re-enactment and living history groups.

Picts and Irish

We do not know by what name the people known as the Picts called themselves, although some have suggested that they knew themselves as the *Cruitui* or *Priteni*. What we do know is that they consisted of a collection of tribes, of whom the *Caledonii* and the *Maeatae* were the largest and possibly the most powerful. As the Roman invasion and subsequent incursions took hold, it would appear that a confederation unified the tribes occupying the land north of the Forth-Clyde line (very roughly, central and north-eastern Scotland). Again, this confederation never labelled itself as Pictish, indeed in later centuries for ease of reference the territory encompassing those tribal lands was often known by the name of

Caledonia, taking its identity from one of the two more dominant tribes. The earliest mention of the Picts was by the classical writer Eumenius in 297 A.D and since his reference to the Picts is a passing one, it seems safe to assume that the term 'Pict' was one which had a definite and well-understood meaning to his audience throughout the Empire. There is no suggestion that the Picts sprang up overnight merely because they are not referred to until the end of the 3rd century. Prior to this reference, the historian Dio

This reconstruction of Pictish costume is based partly on the visual references on the carved symbol stones attributed to the Picts. *Britannia*.

Cassius reported the existence of the *Caledonii* and *Maeatae* in northern Scotland in the early 3rd century, and by referring to these two tribes, confirming their pre-eminence among the many smaller tribes whose names had been recorded (albeit tentatively and sometimes incorrectly) by Claudius Ptolemaeus in his *'Geography'* of circa 150A.D. There is an unreliable reference by Arrian who says that they were *nec falso nomine Pictos* (not falsely named Picts), an oblique statement which might point towards their name being attributable to their body markings, although this is at best an assumption.

By 400A.D. we have the words of Claudian, court poet at the time of Stilicho, suggesting some form of body decoration in his reference to the 'iron-marks' on the bodies of the dying Picts (could this be the same method of tattooing described by Vegetius in his *Epitome of Military Science* when he recommends 'the recruit should not be tattooed with the pin-pricks of the official mark as soon as he has been selected...'?). Obviously the Roman recruits would not have been given the kind of markings which were so definitive an element of the Celtic culture: in this, the Picts had

much in common with the earlier Iron Age peoples of Britain as mentioned by Julius Caesar who refers to the decorated skins of the Britons. In view of the geographical and polical isolation of Caledonia it is is easy to conjecture that this separation contributed towards a slower pace of progress and a stronger hold on traditional practices such as had long been relinquished by their southern British cousins. As a final indication of the nature of the Pictish body markings, we have the words of Isadore of Seville (600A.D.) who explains that the origin of the Picts' name is derived from the fact that they pricked designs into their skins using needles. The obvious problem facing any would-be Pictish re-enactor is that permanent tattooing (even if the designs were right to be based on Pictish symbolism) is perhaps taking authenticity too far, yet to attempt to reproduce the same effect by blue body paint is to run the double risk of either resembling too closely a typical 1st century A.D. Celt or inviting comparison with a romanticized 'noble savage'. In this respect, it may be useful to note

Pictish sword reconstruction, note the simple hilt which has been based on iconographic evidence. The blade is parallel and wide with an obtuse end. The scabbard is purely conjectural and the surface decorations are based on La Tène style patterns. Reconstruction Geoff Maynard.

Recreated Pictish raiders. In the absence of large areas of archaeological information, reliance on iconographic reference is still the best option for equipment reconstruction.

Recreated Pict/Irish raiders engage a later Roman patrol c.400A.D. (Britannia with assistance of J.Nash). Mike Brown English Heritage.

in the re-enactment context that, tempting though it may be to base such designs on the interlaced zoomorphic 'knot-work' so brilliantly executed at its peak in the Book of Kells, this element is not in evidence before the 6th century and hence has no

Dragonesque mount, 7th – 8th Centuries A.D. This piece was found in the Isle of Man and owes more to the Celtic art of the 1st Century than to Roman or even Germanic influence. Nick Nethercoat (after Kilbride Jones).

0   25mm

place on the body of anyone seeking authenticity in the representation of a Pictish warrior up to that watershed date.

Returning to our theme of what we mean by the Picts, they were not a people apart from the other Celtic inhabitants of tribal Scotland. The word 'Picti', meaning 'the painted ones' was coined by Roman soldiers serving on the Empire's most northerly frontier, much in the same derogatory way as European settlers in the old West called the native Americans 'Redskins' despite the latter having many diverse tribal identities by which they knew themselves.

The identity of the Scots or *Scotti* presents similar problems. They are often described as Irish raiders who made the very short sea journey across from Hibernia in their curraghs (hide-covered craft) to join with the Picts, first in raids on the seaboard of the then Roman province of Britannia, and then in permanent settlement on the western side of Scotland, where they often found themselves warring with their some-time allies the Picts. Alternatively there is a view which has gained ground recently that the extension of the kingdom of Dalriada, from Ireland into western Scotland, is not so much confirmation that the *Scotti* came from Ireland in the 5th century to settle in

Argyll but a possible indication that these first Scots although originating in their Highland cradle had reached out in earlier centuries to their neighbours across the Irish sea rather than their tribal cousins to the east because geographically and practically the short sea crossing was easier to undertake than the journey over the mountains to the east of Argyll. Naturally such contacts would foster a cultural closeness which might by the 6th century have made it seem that the Dalriadans owed their identity more to Hibernia than Caledonia. Whatever the true origin of the Scots, we can say that their name seems to derive from the references by Roman writers to 'Scotti', a word which may have its roots in the Irish word for raider or plunderer. Certainly, according to Irish tradition, the sons of Erc, three princes of Dalriada in Antrim, sailed from Ireland to establish kingdoms in Islay, Kintyre and Lorne, all of which lay to the west of the 'Spine of Britain' or the *Dorsum Britanniae* as the 6th century saint and pilgrim Columba calls it. This spine is identified as the mass of mountains from the Grampians up to the north west Highlands, through which there were, and still are, only a few difficult routes. This then is the picture which was the backdrop to the development of the Picts and the Scots.

From this point onwards, because of the scarcity of archaeological evidence, especially of Pictish provenance, we intend to treat the two peoples as one, so linked in their histories that they merged in 843A.D. under the rule of Kenneth mac Alpin, who though king of Dalriada may have had a Pictish mother.

The main obstacles to successful representations of these closely associated peoples through their various Dark Age metamorphoses is the lack of archaeological data and the elusive nature of the Pict/Scot identity; having surmounted those problems, a further pitfall awaits the unwary researcher in that dwelling on the bare essentials (body markings, tribal society with a strong Celtic emphasis and warrior tradition) of the Pictish appearance may result in a romantic Victorian image eclipsing the sum of known facts from reliable sources.

Moving on to firmer ground, it has been suggested that the La Tène style of art and embellishment enjoyed a revival in sub-Roman Britain and Ireland; this idea is supported by finds such as the Clogher

Clogher penannular brooch, 5th-6th Centuries A.D. Decorated with La Tène style swirls. Iain Bell (after Kilbride Jones).

(a,b,c) Pictish symbol design (d) Knot work zoomorphic designs came in after 600A.D. and may owe much to Saxon influence.

A.

B.

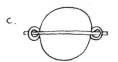

C.

D.

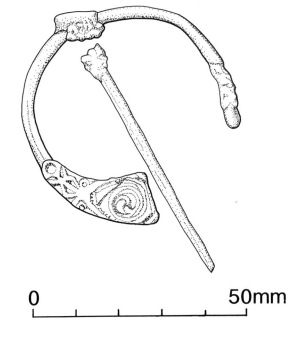

0   50mm

Irish Raider, British coast, 5th century A.D.

The Irish were raiding Britain's coast before the end of Roman rule but the attacks intensified in the 5th century A.D. The Irish or Scots settled in the Argyll area in the later Roman era under their chief Cairbre Riada, this became known as the kingdom of the Dal Riata (Dalriada). The Scots of Dal Riada were thought to have been settled by the British as a mercenary buffer force against the Picts and these Scots were to eventually give their name to the entire region. A mid eighth century Dalriadan document indicates that these Irish colonists were a successful and highly organised naval power capable of organising large land and sea musters.

The vessels of the Scots and indeed the Picts seem to have been hide covered and wooden framed *Curraghs*. These could have been fitted with sails or powered by teams of oarsmen; because of their shallow draughts and low weight they could be taken deep into the bays and rivers of the British coasts.

Irish weapons of the time were generally smaller than the weapons carried by other cultures, the La Tène style persisted in Irish weapon design and manufacture and the evidence suggests a Roman influence in sword development and technology despite no swords of Roman manufacture ever having actually been found in Ireland. Irish swords were to develop little until the Viking incursions in the eighth and ninth centuries. The scabbard chapes that survive amongst the Picts and Irish are rounded and indicate fairy obtuse ends of blades, the chapes themselves may serve a practical purpose, as a blunt and rounded chape would be unlikely to puncture the hide walls of the *Curragh's* hull. The shoes of the main figure are based on surviving examples from the Argyll area. Painting by Richard Hook.

Penannular brooch from Co. Tyrone (decorated in La Tène style swirls and dated to 5th-6th centuries A.D.) and the Celtic-style red enamelled escutcheons on the large hanging bowl of the 7th century Sutton Hoo burial. Coming as they do from two sites so far apart, they may indicate that the resurgence of the La Tène influence was far from localised. Therefore it is quite acceptable to employ the La Tène designs, when depicting Scots and Picts of the sub-Roman era.

This is not to imply that Celtic art had been extinguished in southern Britain under the Roman administration; there are plenty of examples where it was embraced readily by a society greedy for luxury and innovation. So it is feasible that southern British La Tène decorative techniques may have influenced

Re-enactors from *Britannia's* Pictish unit demonstrate what we refer to as the 'Dunnichen battle block'. Lynne Smith.

Kintradwell broch. Already an ancient structure by the time of its 5th century occupation by the Picts. T.E. Gray.

Pictish or Scottish developments as indeed the impact of 400 years of Roman rule continued so to do.

As we have already discussed, the geographic seclusion enjoyed by the Picts and the Scots was certainly an essential factor in the persistence of their culture and we consider that this points towards to the possible continuity of a less diluted style of indigenous decoration. In essence, because of their location and the rugged terrain that protected them, they were not as subject to outside influences as the rest of mainland Britain. This later Celtic style of Ultimate La Tène occurs across a broad spectrum of artefacts, both military and civil, and indeed its eventual fusion with contemporary Germanic art was to result in the ultimate icon of Celtic religious art, the Book of Kells.

Archaeological data on the Picts and the Scots is certainly thin on the ground but not unknown; the written evidence from early chroniclers such as Gildas, Bede, St. Columba and Nennius, provides us with glimpses of the society of both the Picts and the Scots. Other sources of information are the Irish Annals and some of the epics, but the all important surviving visual evidence of the Picts is the most tantalising.

Predictably, Gildas, the 6th century British monk, writes with vitriol about the depredations of the Pictish and Scottish raids: 'As soon as the Romans went back home, there eagerly emerged from the coracles that had carried them across the sea-valleys the foul hordes of the Scots and Picts, like dark throngs of worms who wriggle out of narrow fissures in the rock when the sun is high and the weather grows warm. They were to some extent different in their customs, but they were in perfect accord in their greed for bloodshed: and they were readier to cover their villainous faces with hair than their private parts and neighbouring regions with clothes.'

This long haired and lightly clothed unarmoured warrior image is reinforced to some extent by the aforementioned visual references, notably carved stone symbols or pictograms. These occur throughout many of the regions once dominated by the Picts and there is a recent school of thought which proposes that these highly stylised symbols are not merely religious or ritualistic but may have have more significance in recording aspects of Pictish life, society and even warfare in a hieroglyphic format.

The first symbol stones seem to have appeared in the 6th century; these are undressed slabs with only incised symbols. Following on are slabs from the 8th

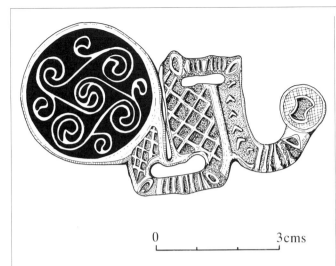

Latchet brooch from Co. Offaly, Ireland. Nick Nethercoat.

century, dressed and with Celtic designs in relief carving. Another later classification of stones describes those with Celtic relief carving but no symbols, which were erected in the 9th and 10th centuries, after the Scots conquest of the Picts. This classification made by Dr J. Anderson in 1903 still holds good today, and is relevant because it enables us to extrapolate visual elements from the monuments and use them in the correct time period.

From these sources we have attempted basic reconstructions of Pictish wargear in the sub-Roman Early Saxon era, remembering that the stones in particular may represent a two way traffic in artistic influence between Anglian Northumbria and Celtic Caledonia.

Helmets

Helmets present would-be Pictish re-enactors with the age-old problem of personal safety over accuracy; whilst it can be argued quite realistically that Pictish warriors may have plundered their dead foes for arms and armour, there is little to suggest that helmets or indeed body armour were ever worn by them. No example of Pictish protective headgear has ever been archaeologically substantiated, not even a single helmet component is available for study. The subject of headgear and body armour has been explored in some detail by Graeme Cruickshank (Pictish Arts Society Journal 5, 1994, *Did the Picts wear helmets?*). In this well argued article he highlights two possible references to Pictish war helmets. The first is iconographic in the form of the incised stone illustration of what could possibly be a conical *spangenhelm* (segmented helmet) on the Balbair stone, assuming that it depicts a Pictish warrior. Mr Cruickshank refers to J. Romilly Allen's comment on the bird-like rendition of a warrior's head and says that

the 'beak-like shape does bear a superficial resemblance to the badly-drawn helmets in Alexander Gordon's sketch of the Aberlemno Stone, published in 1726. Nevertheless, just what the sculptor intended this curious appendage to represent must remain open to question'. William Jolly commented in 1882 that 'some of the lines on the stone, especially those about the mouth and head, are somewhat difficult to make out, and may give rise to different renderings of the figure.' Mr Cruickshank concludes: 'This is indeed what has happened, for published sketches show the "Beak/helmet" element in a variety of guises, while in those based on rubbings, the feature simply fades away. All things considered, it cannot be said with any degree of assurance that Balblair man is wearing a helmet'. All of which is very disappointing for the re-enactor.

Cruickshank's second reference to a possible Pictish helmet is part of what he quite correctly refers to as 'one of the saddest episodes in Scottish antiquarianism'. The Norries Law hoard was removed from a tumulus in Fife around 1819 by workmen digging for sand, and a large part of the hoard was sold off for its bullion value; only a handful of the items

Irish sword, Ultimate La Tène style, from Co. Offaly Ireland.

Dan Shadrake.

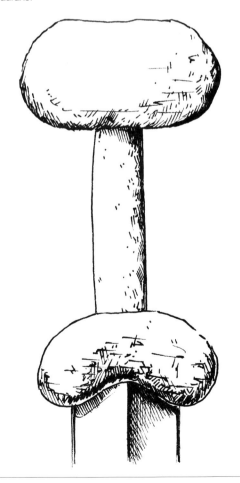

The Drosten crossbowman re-created. The crossbow is of an elementary design and has a rising peg trigger and wooden prod (Chris Pegley of _Britannia's_ Pictish unit). Lynne Smith.

were saved and donated to the National Museum of Antiquities of Scotland. The decoration of the remaining objects is quite definitely Pictish in its execution; because of the illicit way that the rest of the hoard was disposed of no first hand record was made of the missing artefacts. Around 20 years after its discovery George Buist attempted to compile a report on the Norries Law hoard to the Fifeshire Literary and Antiquarian Society, using what he referred to as 'the insecure treasury of oral tradition'. His task was a difficult one and much of the report is speculative such as the 'rich coat of scale-armour, the pieces of which consisted of small-sized lozenge-shaped plates of silver, suspended loosely by a hook from the upper corner.' This seems a highly unlikely description of scale armour, construction and configuration when all other such finds are considered, and a little later Buist's interpretation of this type of armour was refuted in the Archaeological Journal of 1849 by Albert Way who pointed out that the surviving scales were unperforated and therefore had no means of suspension or attachment to a backing garment. Other

items said to have been present in the hoard were a decorated shield, a sword hilt, and, of course, a helmet. Local folklore had it that a warrior was buried in the mound in a full suit of armour and Buist was to call his report _The Silver Armour of Norries Law_.

According to Buist's report these items were 'when found, quite entire, but they were crushed into pieces to permit convenient transport and concealment'. The jeweller involved in the sad business of melting down these treasures was able to recall the details of much of the armour for Buist and illustrations were made depicting nine of the objects but some of them are dubiously rendered and seem to owe more to high medieval art than ancient Pictish embellishment (particularly the sword hilt). The helmet does not appear to have been included in this set of illustrations and (if indeed it did exist) one can only speculate as to its appearance – perhaps a gilded silver, later Romano-Sassanian style helmet such as the Deurne example from Holland? Alternatively, an embryonic Coppergate-style Northumbrian helmet taken in battle and adapted for an unknown Pictish warlord would not be beyond the bounds of archaeological plausibility.

Cruickshank points out that 'the little we know of the Norries Law hoard, it is clear that any martial content was concerned with ceremonial activities, not actual warfare, and so the silver helmet should not be taken as an indication that the Picts wore helmets in battle. Moreover, the lack of corroboration regarding the missing items from Norries Law renders the account of the helmet of dubious value to any discussion on Pictish helmets. Thus we are left without any concrete evidence that the Picts ever wore helmets.'

All we can safely say is that despite numerous depictions of warriors on these stones, they represent both the fully helmeted enemy (not always identifiable) and warriors we must take to be Pictish, whose headgear on closer inspection is almost invariably a stylised representation of hair, usually shown as swept back and quite long. So the matter of Pictish helmets is open and awaits further discoveries.

Swords

We are better served in the matter of swords, particularly as there are enough early Dark Age examples from Irish sites to warrant categorisation, and which correspond to depictions of swords on Pictish standing stones, so that it is quite reasonable to

Bottom left and right.
Replicas of early Irish shoes made by Ivor and Simone Lawton of *Dawn of Time Crafts*.

assert that they echo each other and that when we look at the Irish swords we can say that we are looking at Pictish swords. Although the Irish swords have different elements, they share one common characteristic, and that is their size. Invariably they are shorter than their Germanic counterparts, and this is a hallmark of Irish origins. Even the longest of these Irish swords measures only 66cms in total length. The 4th to 5th century blades in this group are lozenge-shaped or have three ribs or channels, although it must be said that the latter variety have never been found to occur in Britain.

The background to Pictish/Scottish swords must therefore be considered in the light of the persistence of the La Tène culture in Ireland, as we have already outlined, and to some extent in the homelands of the Caledonian Picts and the Dalriadan Scots, areas which we would now tend to designate the 'Celtic fringes'. The La Tène movement, having exhausted itself in the rest of Europe and having been swept aside by new fashions in weapons design and technology, especially from the expanding Germanic peoples, was effectively preserved in a kind of timewarp. In this hidden society, swords developed at a slower rate. A good example of late, or Ultimate La Tène was found in Edenberry, Co. Offaly in Ireland; this was dated to the 3rd – 4th centuries A.D. and the hilt had the distinct rounded

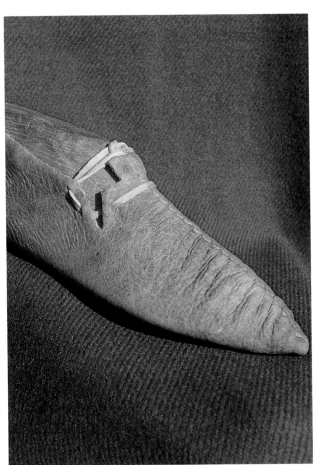

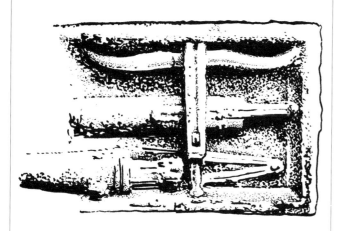

Eastern Roman crossbow. Dan Shadrake.

organic traits of the La Tène culture. However, Roman influence was to finally overtake the La Tène style in Irish sword manufacture and despite no Roman sword ever having been found in Ireland there are several good examples of the smaller Irish style *spatha* and *gladius*. These swords persisted in Ireland well into the 8th century A.D. as there was to be little in the way of large-scale outside military pressure until

The Drosten stone (8th-9th Century) depicts a hunter with a crossbow. T. E. Gray.

the Norse raiding and colonisation.

As for Pictish swords, the best evidence is sadly pictoral, the hilts represented on the swords of warriors depicted on the early stones are shown as having broad parallel blades that terminate in an obtuse point. The hilts are modest and the guards are often represented as two slight simple curves that face away from the hand grip. These visual representations are not unlike the surviving archaeological examples from Ireland and serve as a possible indicator of how closely the cultures of the Picts and the Scots were linked. Only one fragment of sword that has been tentatively identified as Pictish survives, although this was found in Dunadd, which was thought to have been the Duinatt of the early medieval era, an important stronghold for the Dalriadic Scots. The 14cm long fragment was the obtuse iron tip of a parallel sided sword that had a blade width of 5cm. The blade had a central ridge or spine, which judging by the surviving component ran from the hilt to the point. The St. Ninian's Isle treasure contained finely worked silver scabbard chapes that were based on double headed serpents; these had been inscribed with a Pictish name using Irish lettering and have been dated to around 800A.D. These are interesting and enigmatic objects as the swords and scabbards are absent and we can only speculate as to their appearance but they do seem

to belong to swords that were distinctly blunt tipped. Three figures on the Birsay stone (Orkney Islands) have scabbards slung from their waist belts. Although the hilt details are sadly obscured from view, the scabbard ends are quite visible and all seem to be bearing parallel sided swords with blunt tips.

Reconstructions of Pictish swords of the 4th to 6th centuries could vary considerably considering the lack of archaeological evidence and the massive areas that are open to interpretation and invention. The curious thing is that most serious attempts to reconstruct these weapons have resulted in strikingly similar conclusions, even though there is no indication that the individuals and groups that have attempted reconstructions have conferred or used the same evidence or taken the same paths to their ultimate conclusions. The lack of surviving data for crossguards has been put down to their construction of either organic material or ferrous metal, since there is also a lack of surviving evidence for blades, the latter is quite an acceptable option. The most popular Pictish or Scottish weapon reconstruction favoured by the clients of modern armourers has been a wide bladed, blunt tipped sword with a plain black iron effect hilt, (blades of this style are designed for hacking rather than thrusting).

War Axes

Small hand axes were found at the Dunadd excavations but these were thought to have been little more than craft tools. A stone carving dated at around the 6th to 7th century shows a figure holding an axe in two hands by its long thin haft; the pose of the figure suggests that it is a battle axe and not a utilitarian tool. The lack of archaeological evidence, however, means that we can draw no conclusions from this image but its resemblance to the long battle axe of the contemporary Sutton Hoo burial is rather interesting despite the geographical separation of these two areas of evidence.

Spears

Excavations in what is thought to have been the Dalriadic stronghold at Dunadd reveal small, unremarkable spearheads, the largest being around 10cms long. This seems to relate well to the visual references found on examples of Pictish art such as the

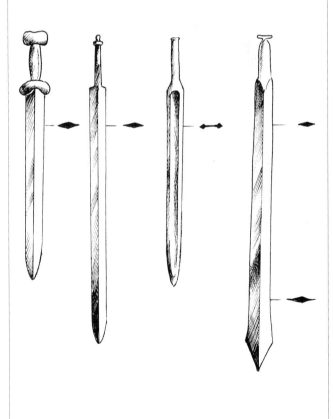

Sword blades of the Pre-Viking Irish Warrior, 4th to 8th centuries A.D. (from Etienne Rynne's Classification of Pre-Viking Irish Iron Swords).

Peter Faulkner's curragh with crew. The Scotsman Magazine.

Aberlemno churchyard stone. The three figures on the Birsay stone appear to be bearing broad headed spears on thick shafts. The archaeological evidence for Irish spears of the early Dark Age suggests a modest variety of heads, the Irish epic *The Tain* (tran. Thomas Kinsella, Oxford University Press, 1969) describes an army assembling: 'Tunics covered them to the knee. They carried full length shields and each man had a broad grey stabbing spear on a slender shaft' Much of the *Tain* is wild exaggeration and understandably so given that it is heroic and epic in nature, but such basic elements such as the above description are unlikely to have been altered significantly, and as with contemporary cultures the spear was the most common weapon of the rank and file.

Spear shafts could be made from a variety of indigenous woods; the Scots pine is a very ancient variety and it has a slightly more dense grain than the other strains of pine. The Picts and Scots would have undoubtedly used this wood for spear shafts, along with oak, hornbeam and ash.

Excavations on Iona have revealed evidence for wood turning and the pole lathes could certainly be used to produce spear shafts, but a passage from St Columba refers to an Irish layman named Gore who 'chanced one day to be sitting beneath a boat, shaving the bark off a spear shaft with his own knife'. (*The Illustrated Life of St Columba*, J. Marsden, Floris books, 1991). This practice of shaving the bark off a spear shaft may be an indication of coppicing to provide the warrior society with a regular stock of spear shafts, axe hafts and shield wood.

Shields

Pictish shields of the early Dark Ages are widely represented on their stone sculptures. Most of the images are small round targes, that are shown with or without central bosses. No archaeological examples of Pictish shields remain and the few shield bosses that survive the early Dark Ages in Ireland are tiny (5cm high dome, 11cm wide boss). These seem appropriate in size when the smaller Irish facsimiles of Roman weapons are considered. The Birsay stone (Orkney Is) has three figures that are represented as carrying square targes. All three are shown as having surface decorations and thick edging. If such shields were indeed used for battle we would suggest that the thick edging bands depicted are strips of rawhide (used as shield rim protection), the surface decoration may be designs that were pressed or painted onto a leather and fabric surface.

The Aberlemno churchyard stone (dated to the last half of the 7th century) has a variety of shields represented on it. This is widely thought to be a representation of the Pictish victory over the Northumbrians at the battle of Nechtansmere (also known as Dunnichen) fought in the spring of 685A.D. Two opposing forces are depicted on what is interpreted as a battle scene. The warriors on the left side of the stone are thought to represent the Pictish forces; all these warriors are bare-headed and have pointed beards. The mounted warriors on the right side of the stone are shown wearing helmets that are similar to the depictions on the Frank's casket and the archaeological evidence of the Coppergate helmet, and are thought to represent the Northumbrian army.

The mounted Northumbrians have small, flat circular shields (from hand to elbow length) and are carrying stabbing spears, and the mounted Picts seem to be protecting infantry flanks, thus it is easy to interpret the Aberlemno stone as a battle plan. The three infantrymen depicted are thought to represent the central block of infantry and their arrangement in profile is thought to be a clear indicator of how the

Peter Faulkner's curragh reconstruction. The Scotsman Magazine.

Picts under King Bruide used a disciplined formation that seems to owe more to the principles of classical warfare than the mad onslaught normally associated with Celtic warriors.

If this image is indeed to be taken as a battle formation, then the first warrior (in the front Pictish line) is bearing a slashing *spatha*-style sword and small bossed, gripped shield; presumably it would be his function to hack away at those members of the opposing force who got inside the reach of the Pictish long spears (borne horizontally by the second rank). This second rank spearman seems to have a large shoulder slung shield, which would give him the ability to manoeuvre his spear with both hands whilst protecting the entire left side of his upper body. The third rank spearman stands at the ready but is not in a combat pose. The stance of the third person may be a further indication that this is a cross section of a Pictish battle formation, as experience in early Dark Age battle re-enactment will show that due to the nature of weapons and the style of fighting, the third row in a block of warriors rarely gets the chance to engage the enemy directly (not counting projectiles), and is present in a reserve role. The more manpower in the formation the more it is possible to give a force sufficient bulk and to stab at the enemy who make it through the first two lines, thus preventing their

64 Picts and Irish

advance and literally to fill dead men's shoes.

Britannia's Pictish section recreated this formation, which we shall term the Dunnichen battle block, with great effect against random and ordered forces of greater number; our conclusions were that, providing order is kept, this formation is very hard to beat, as it has both the advantages of spear reach and manoeuvrability of close quarter engagement. This would make it an effective formation to use against cavalry and infantry.

Projectiles

It is likely that the Picts employed the use of both archery and sling-shot but the absence of evidence in this area makes any further commentary impossible. Gildas in his *De Excidio Britonum* states that throwing spears were used by the Picts against the British stationed at Hadrian's Wall: 'there was no respite from the barbed spears flung by their naked opponents, which tore our wretched countrymen from the walls and dashed them to the ground.'

The Drosten stone (8th-9th century A.D.) depicts a hunter carrying what is obviously a crossbow. This is perhaps more readily associated with later time periods and has often been dismissed as a hunting tool, having little military value in early contexts. In choosing to include one in our presentations that involve Pictish raiders, *Britannia* runs the risk of looking anachronistic but one must also consider the much earlier depiction of a Roman crossbow on a 2nd-3rd century relief carving which also shows a dagger and tubular shaped quiver (Museum Crozatier, Le Puy).

Leather Work

Excavations on Iona revealed a variety of leather fragments, these included half of a square cowhide purse (110mm x 95mm) and some leather shoe uppers. These fragments of 'turned shoes' are similar to late Roman designs but some have the curious addition of elongated heel stiffeners that have no contemporary parallels.

Sea-Borne Raids

We know from sources such as Gildas that the Picts and the Scots used hide boats to raid Britain, and the kingdom of the Dalriadic Scots consisted of a portion of north east Ireland as well as some of the islands and part of the mainland of south west Scotland. Their success as the dominant military force that was to

Pictish spearhead.

eventually overcome the Picts must have depended largely on their ability as a naval power, especially when one considers that a larger part of their kingdom was separated by the open sea.

The evidence for the appearance of these *curraghs* or hide ships is quite thin on the ground; there are plenty of references to ships being carried by men in both Adamnan's *Life of Columba* and the writings of St Patrick, indicating light-framed vessels. Ships with sails are occasionally mentioned, although it is not clear if the ships in question are constructed from hides or are clinker built. A gold model of what appears to be a hide covered boat (1st century A.D.) was found in Broighter Co. Derry, and this is fitted with a set of oars and a mast.

Recent *curragh* reconstructions have been successfully attempted by the Shropshire based coracle maker Peter Faulkner. He used 'thumb thick' hazel rods and employed a method called 'open mouth waling' (a weaving technique used by basket makers). Thirty six stout rods were inserted into the ground in the shape of the boat desired; these were then bent over and lashed together using heavy duty twine that was made of hemp and dressed in tar. The rods were woven together at the mouth or rim. This formed the basic structure of the boat on to which the hide skin was stitched. The selected cow hides were checked for flaws, immersed in a saline bath for ten days and then washed with fresh water and allowed to drain until they were in a soft pliable state.

A total of three full-size cowhides were used, which were stitched together down two 7 inch seams using traditional awls and needles; the leather off-cuts were used to lash the sewn hides to the framework. The whole process of construction took seven days and the result was a vessel that one could easily imagine being used by the Picts and Scots raiders 1,400 years ago.

Saxons

Although the 2nd century Roman writer Ptolemy is the first to mention the Saxons as a people in his *Geography*, there are earlier references by Tacitus to Germanic people of the first century A.D., in particular to their methods of warfare: 'Only a few of their number carry swords or spears with metal heads. As a rule they carry spears capped with a short and

Recreated Germanic noble. Much of his equipment is either of Roman manufacture or at least heavily influenced by Roman fashion. His lamellar cuirass is made from laquered rawhide and is based on 5th-6th century iron examples found in Frankish graves. His helmet is based on the Vendel grave (South Sweden) helmets of the 6th century.

narrow metal point, the weapon is so handy that it can be used to spike as well as to throw. Cavalry carries only shield and spear. Those on foot also carry missiles (i.e. slingers). The Germans enter battle bare chested or, at the most are clad in a light cover which hinders them little in their movement. Far removed from them is any idea to shine in the splendour of their weapons. Only their shields are painted in glaring colours.'

Despite these references it would seem that the Saxons as a people had little or no impact on the Roman Empire until the 3rd century. Of course the Germanic peoples played their part as auxiliaries within the Roman army and in this way their culture was seeded, their traditions and to some extent their accoutrements were disseminated throughout the reaches of the Empire. By the third century the Saxons had embarked on an ever increasing pattern of harrassment, particularly of the coasts of western Europe and Britain. By the 4th century this harrassment had intensified into rapacious assaults, particularly on Britain and Gaul, with the inevitable result of the establishment of settlements.

With the breakdown of the administration and very fabric of the Roman Empire, yet more Saxons continued this movement into the eastern part of Britain, rightly perceiving it to be rich and easy pickings. The 5th century poet, later bishop, Sidonius Apollinaris, who as a landowner had good reason to take an interest in their raids described them as outdoing all others in brutality; he went on to say they were ungovernable, entirely at home at sea, and that they attacked unexpectedly – this has marked similarities to the words of the 8th and 9th century chroniclers describing the Viking raids. Interestingly, as Sidonius was writing from his lands in Aquitaine in about 470 A.D., the marauders he talks of could, by this time, easily have been Saxons using Britain as a base for their predatory attacks on Europe.

Set alongside these incursions is a fact that we

Recreated Saxon raiders (Britannia). M. Clow.

have already mentioned, that of the overwhelming evidence showing the presence of Germanic units of soldiers serving in the Roman army in Britain prior to the 4th century. Inscriptions found at Burgh (Cumbria), Housesteads (Hadrian's Wall) and Binchester (Durham) attest to the presence of at least three cavalry units of Frisians. The presence of the *cuneus Frisionum Aballavensium* is indicated by two inscriptions dated to around A.D. 241-249, one of which reads IN C[U]NEUM FRISIONUM ABALLAVENSIUM (meaning 'to the formation of Frisians of Aballava'), the formation in this case being the *cuneus* or cavalry unit of a regiment. The second cavalry unit's existence at Housesteads is confirmed by an inscription on an altar set up by the GER[MANI] CIVES TUIHANTI CUNEI FRISIORUM VER [COVICIANORUM] and this is worthy of comment as it seems to refer to the citizen as being 'Germani'; this has been dated circa 225.A.D.

The presence of the 3rd cavalry unit of Frisians at Binchester is confirmed by an altar set up by a soldier who was EX C[UNEO] FRIS[IORUM] VINOVIE[NSIUM]. All three were raised from the Frisii of Holland, a Germanic people occuping the

areas that are now northern Holland and the coastal lands of northern Germany. A further example of Germanic troops in Britain can be found, again at Housesteads, where a third century inscription refers to the NUMERUS HNAUDIFRIDI, a regiment raised in Germany and named after its commander *Hnaudifridus*.

Furthermore, Ammianus Marcellinus in his *'History'* refers to an episode in the time of Valentinian (372A.D.) 'when an invasion devastated Britain, he gave Fraomarius the rank of tribune and sent him off to Britain with a troop of the Alemanni – at that time the tribe was noted for its size and strength.' To complete the evidence for a strong Germanic presence at all levels in the Roman army, there are the examples of Nectaridus and Fullofaudes, both Germans and both high ranking officers serving in Britain's Roman army; ironically both were victims of hostile sea raiders.

Despite this evidence, the traditional view that large waves of rampaging Germanic mercenaries first entered a weakened and unstable Britain at the request of the British leader Vortigern owes much to popular misconception. There have been many romantic and legendary versions of this story but these events are partly true and reflect just one reason amongst many

A recreated warrior of Germanic origin in the 4th Century A.D. Roman army. John Eagle.

why the Germanic incursions were so successful that the chief language of the British Isles today owes more to the peoples of the Low countries than the Romano-Celtic cultures.

What is certain is that the raids and incursions intensified in the 4th and 5th centuries, putting greater pressure on the indigenous population, the most likely explanation for this new tide of incomers is given by Gildas in his *De excidio Britonum* when he says 'And they [the British rulers] convened a council to decide the best and soundest way to counter the brutal and repeated invasions and plunderings by the peoples I have mentioned [these are the 'the old enemies' the Scottii and Pictii]. Then all the members of the council, together with the proud tyrant, were struck blind; the guard – or rather the method of destruction – they devised for our land was that the ferocious Saxons (name not to be spoken!), hated by man and God, should be let into the island like wolves into the fold, to beat back the peoples of the north. Nothing more destructive, nothing more bitter has ever befallen the land. How utter the blindness of their

The Benty Grange helmet. *Sheffield City Museum.*

The Coppergate helmet. York Archaeological Trust.

minds! how desperate and crass the stupidity! Of their own free will they invited under the same roof a people whom they feared worse than death even in their absence!'

By the 6th century, 'Saxon' was a very general term applying to an unstructured grouping of Germanic peoples whose lands lay to the north of Germany roughly between Mecklenburg and Frisia or between the Elbe and Weser rivers; this is not to imply any form of confederation, they were led by individual nobles whose main business was warfare. It is these peoples who are traditionally credited with conquering southern and eastern Britain following the collapse of the Roman Empire. Despite the rather jaundiced accounts by Gildas, the earliest reliable narrative of this chapter in British history is the *Historia Ecclesiastica Gentis Anglorum* (Ecclesiastical History of the English People), completed by the monk Bede in 731 A.D.

In this work Bede refers to the English newcomers as coming from 'the three most formidable races of Germany, the Saxons, Angles and Jutes... From the

Angles, that is a country known as Angulus, which lies between the provinces of the Jutes and Saxons and is said to remain unpopulated to this day, are descended the East and the Middle Angles, the Mercians, all the Northumbrian stock'. This is a little simplified as other waves of Germanic invaders were to leave their mark on the archaeology and culture of the developing British Isles, the Frisians, the Carolingians and the Suebians amongst them.

The legacy of Germanic settlement in Britain is perhaps most obvious in the survival of the names of seven ancient kingdoms as modern county and regional names – Essex, Wessex, Sussex, Northumbria, East Anglia, Kent and Mercia, but also in the very language used by the majority of people in south Britain today.

The attractions of migration era Germanic military equipment for a growing number of re-enactors, model makers, and historians are not only the diversity of weapons and armour and the large amounts of information available, but also the massive cultural impact that the Romans had on the Saxons,

Merovingians, Frisians, Angles and Jutes, together with the undeniable and far reaching effect that these people had on the Roman world. The inevitable fusion of Roman and Germanic hardware provides the enthusiast with a great opportunity to be creative without leaving the realms of realism.

A wealth of reference, from the unadorned and functional to the highly embellished and ceremonial, gives us the most fascinating aspect of this fusion – the survival of classical elements into Germanic military technology and general decoration. It is well known that the Romans had a practice of hiring mercenaries (*laeti*) or settling pro- Roman barbarians into weakened fringes of the Empire in return for military service (*foederati*). It was inevitable that Roman equipment, and practices would have found their way in to the Germanic military milieu; this exchange worked both ways.

This persistence of the Roman style amongst the later Germanic warriors is highlighted by archaeological evidence in areas of northern Europe outside the Empire's borders. The Nydam and Vimose ship burials and an abundance of grave goods in north Germany and south Scandinavia display objects with heavy Roman influence or Roman manufacture. Roman objects such as coins were often grafted into Germanic jewellery, and some examples betray

Interpretation of the 'Confessor' helmet, the modern armourer has used the dotted pattern on the brow-band as a decorative feature in this convincing reconstruction. Made by Ivor Lawton of *Dawn of Time Crafts*.

Recreated Northumbrian warrior, 7th century. He is wearing a basic Coppergate style helmet. G. Lee.

Replica of the Benty Grange helmet made by Martin Murphy. *Sheffield City Museum.*

attempts to reproduce Roman objects and images in their own less naturalistic but no less attractive fashion.

By this time, the Germanic tribes had come to provide a large proportion of the manpower required by the Roman army in the west, particularly being stationed in northern Gaul for some considerable time. The Eastern Roman writer Procopius wrote about the continuation of Roman military customs amongst the Germanic *Arborychi* of northern Gaul. Less than two centuries earlier than Procopius, Sidonius Apollinaris described the 'gracious sight' of the Frankish prince Sigismer and his companions travelling to meet his bride: 'Their swords suspended from the shoulders by baldrics pressed against their sides girded with studded deer skins. This equipment adorned and armed them at the same time. Barbed lances and throwing axes filled their right hands; and their left sides were protected by shields, the gleam of which, golden on the cental bosses and silvery white around the rims, betrayed at once the wearers' wealth and ruling passion'.

These writers describe in a very favourable light

and very useful detail the pro-Roman Germanic forces, although not all early writers share this same enthusiasm for the northern barbarians. In fact, Vegetius *(Epitome of Military Science)* concedes that the 'peoples from the North are readiest for wars' but credits them with less intelligence, being 'remote from the sun's heat'.

The archaeological evidence for the persistence of Roman culture is plentiful and widespread but the important question is at what point does one cease to portray late Roman militia and begin to portray the Saxon which followed it. In re-enactment terms there is no simple answer to this question as there was no simple ending to the Roman era or an exact commencement for the Saxon period. This ambiguity of cultural identity is occasionally reflected in the archaeology. For instance, the persistence of the undeniably late Roman style of the 'Ridge' helmet underpinning the helmets of the Sutton Hoo and Vendel graves (see Viking chapter), the endurance of the *spatha*-style long sword well into the Saxon era, and the curious seated figure represented on the lid of a 5th century Saxon cremation urn from Spong Hill

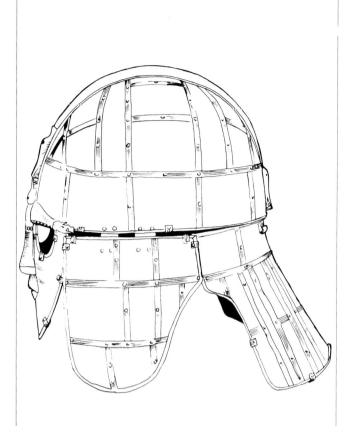

The Sutton Hoo helmet. Dan Shadrake.

which has what appears to be a Pannonian or 'pillbox' hat (a popular item of headgear amongst the late Romans), all indicate a mixture of cultures.

This chronological confusion is perhaps more acute in the late Roman/early Saxon era than in any other. Radiocarbon dating (the method of dating objects by the decay of carbon) isn't always precise to the nearest year or even decade, and as Leslie Alcock in *Arthur's Britain* points out, one has to allow for a discrepancy of 70 years either side of the estimated date. In this chapter we shall be discussing military equipment from 410-1066 A.D.

Helmets

Only three archaeological examples of helmets survive the Saxon era (between the end of Roman administration and the Battle of Hastings) in Britain. Despite its widespread contemporary artistic representation, the one-piece conical and the segmented *spangenhelm* are curiously absent from find sites. Depictions on carvings, manuscripts, coins and of course the Bayeux Tapestry indicate that the single piece and segmented conical were widely used, at least amongst the English warrior elite in a late

Saxon context.

All three Saxon helmets found in Britain belong to the 'Ridge' helmet classification; the first of these examples we shall concentrate on is the Benty Grange helmet (this was found in a burial barrow by Thomas Bateman at Benty Grange, Derbyshire in 1848). From the remaining data and impressions left in the corrosion on the reinforcing iron bands, Bateman suggested that the segments between those supporting bands were composed of a herringbone pattern of horn plates over which large strips of vertical horn were fixed. Horn, like wood has strata or a grain running through it, and, like wood, can be made flexible and workable by simple processes of immersion. This would have provided a lightweight but durable alternative to metal, and if Bateman was correct about the layered horn configuration, then it seems the these plates were arranged with the grain running at different angles (in much the same way that plywood is made), for strength and flexibility. Bateman also noted other points such as the rivets that originally held the horn plates to the iron bands being coated in silver heads, and a silver cross on the noseguard as well as the boar on the crest he described as 'a good representation of a pig'. Subsequent and detailed examination by the British Museum has yielded a more specific report on the helmet and its components, most notably the boar on the crest. Cleaning the boar revealed that it was rendered with surprisingly life-like proportions, composed of many complex parts, not cast as a solid piece. The legs of this creature were made of iron which were then applied to flanks that were also made of iron. The boar's body was hollow and composed of two equal copper-alloy halves, and had eyes made of garnet secured in gold mounts. The surface of the body was set with silver studs and had hip plates that were gilded, as well as carefully cast copper-alloy ears, tail, and tusks. Perhaps the the most interesting features are the decoration on the boar's underbelly which was made using Roman silver, and the 2mm slit running the length of the boar's back, which has been suggested was a mount for a real crest of horse hair or indeed boar bristles, perhaps echoing the crests of earlier Roman helmets, whose visual representation at least must have survived to the time of the Benty Grange helmet. In 1986 a replica of the Benty Grange helmet was made by Martin Murphy. He chose materials similar to those used in the production of the original, and the result was a lightweight but strong helmet. Murphy attributes these qualities to the choice of horn and the hollow construction of the boar. He also states that the horn plates 'cannot be split easily with an axe or sword'. He also noted that the mercury gilding process used on the silver and copper alloy (bronze) components produced enough heat to give the iron a blue-black hue, which he shows would act as the perfect background for the silver and gilt decoration and which is not unlike the natural colouring of the wild boar, incidentally itself a possibly totemic animal to the Saxons as well as to the earlier Celts. The Benty Grange helmet is the only example that has a boar intact or perhaps we should say it is the only boar that has been found and associated with with the remains of a helmet, since separate boars similar to this one have been identified minus any remains of a helmet bowl.

The Benty Grange helmet has been tentatively dated to the late 6th-early 7th century and this style of helmet may have been mentioned in the early Saxon poem *Beowulf*: 'where the bound blade cuts, with its sharp edges shining with blood, through the boars that bristle above the foes' helmets!'

The second crested (or 'Ridge') helmet found in Britain from the burial mound at Sutton Hoo is perhaps the best known find of the pre-Norman Conquest period. It could also conform to another helmet that was described in *Beowulf as* having a 'comb

passing over the roof of the helmet wound around with wire inlay'. The Sutton Hoo helmet has indeed got a raised comb or crest that is inlaid with silver wire and terminates at both ends with highly styilized animal heads. This decorative component and overall construction has, so far, no surviving British contemporaries but striking parallels are to be seen in the Vendel and Valsgärde graves of Sweden (see Viking chapter). Interestingly enough, the Vendel and Valsgärde finds were contemporary with the south Swedish Geats, who were the people described in *Beowulf!*

The Sutton Hoo helmet (excavated by B. Brown and E. Pretty in 1938) has been dated to the 7th century but may have earlier roots. Its construction is considered to have an obvious basis in the late Roman 'Ridge' helmet, if not in the actual manufacture of underlying components then at least in influence. Like many Roman ridge helmets it comprised an iron bowl fixed to a ridge or crest of metal, cheek and neck guards hung from the bowl; the whole iron surface of the helmet was covered in thin copper alloy plates that had been stamped with intricate motifs (4 different designs were identified). These were held in place by copper-alloy strips and

Deurne Helmet. Mandy Turner.

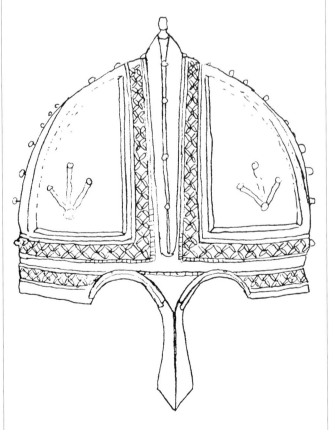

Coin of Edward the Confessor, depicting a conical helmet.

A diversity of equipment is available to the 5th century Germanic re-enactor. Here members of the *Milites Litoris Saxonici* demonstrate a successful fusion of 'barbarian' and classical influences. D. Clow.

rivets that appear to accentuate the panels. The eyebrows are cast copper-alloy (bronze) and terminate in cast boar heads. The face guard was also constructed of iron and is decorated with stamped, tinned copper-alloy sheets as well as the applied components of a nose, mouth and moustache. The Sutton Hoo helmet is normally thought of as a ceremonial helmet or even death mask with no place on the battlefield. The rich embellishment is one reason for this theory, but considering the frequency of surviving late Roman examples of richly decorated helmets from Budapest, Berkasovo and Deurne, not to mention the highly embellished but battle worthy helmets of later periods (Europe's Renaissance armies, Napoleon's Imperial Guard for instance), one cannot exclude the possibility of a helmet's use on the battlefield because of its surface decoration, although such a fine object would only be worn by the highest ranking personnel.

The face mask and heavy neck and cheek guards are other factors in favour of this helmet being dismissed as having any practical use in a skirmish or battle scenario; the popular theory is that they would have impaired the wearer's vision. However, one must consider the style of infantry warfare in late Roman and early Saxon Britain, which tends to be one of initial missile exchange followed by tightly packed shield formations, pushing for supremacy against each other and employing edged weapons, mainly spears and swords to that end. From the experience of re-enacting this style of warfare, when one is caught up in a melée of this description, it is often the case that movement is restricted to such a degree that one's shield and weapons are often effectively pinned down, leaving the head vulnerable to missile fire and unlucky 'jabs' from the rear ranks of enemy spearmen. A helmet offering protection against such an attack would be of primary importance since the necessity of a large field of vision would be secondary to the protective values it offered in conflicts of this type. It would in our opinion be rash to dismiss, if not the Sutton Hoo helmet, then a more functional version of this helmet, from having been used in early Saxon conflicts, despite its apparent over-ornamentation.

The third surviving crested helmet from Saxon Britain is the recently discovered Coppergate helmet (York 1986). Like the other crested helmets, the dome of this helmet was constructed from iron components. A broad strip of iron that incorporated the foundation for the nasal was riveted to a wide brow-band creating a flat crest that ran from the front of the helmet to the back. Broad supporting side struts were, in turn, riveted either side of the flat crest and then fixed to the brow-band, which in turn formed a cross-braced frame to which four inner segments were fixed (riveted to the inside by approx 11-12 rivets each). The methods of construction of the Coppergate's bowl are similar to the Swedish Valsgärde helmet, although much of the copper alloy embellishment is unique to this find. The most interesting features are the long nasal (basic reconstructions prove that this adds to the protective value), the rebated eyebrows and 'semi-crescent' cheek guards which increase the wearer's protection without compromising his field of vision. The cheek guards are edged with a fine 'piping' of copper alloy which is slightly reminiscent of the fine edging given to the cheek guards of earlier Roman helmets, although the only connection here is in the quality of workmanship. These cheekguards are suspended from the browband of the dome by means of a simple hinge, and fixed to both cheekguards and brow-band is the remarkably well preserved mail aventail. The links of this aventail were made of 1mm iron wire and were riveted closed, their diameter is

7.7-7.9mm. This aventail is another feature that highlights close parallels between the Coppergate helmet and its counterparts in Valsgärde and Vendel cultures having aventails of similar gauge mail links. These continental helmets are dated to the 7th century, although the Coppergate has been dated as late as the mid 8th century, and considering the chronology and location of this find, coupled with representations on the Franks' casket and the Aberlemno stone (see the chapter on the Picts), it is quite likely to be Northumbrian in origin.

The archaeological evidence for later Saxon helmets is almost non-existent and so the same principles employed in the recreation of later Viking helmets have to be used. Visual information from carvings, manuscripts, frescoes and the written word, and as we have already discussed, numismatic sources (images on coins) can all be employed; for the obvious reasons this has certain drawbacks and without supporting archaeological data an interpretation of headgear or indeed any other item of armour or equipment can be easily be disputed as being based on nothing more than the classical tendencies or wild imaginations of a long dead artisan.

Some Saxon manuscripts depict warriors dressed in an eclectic mixture of contemporary Saxon clothing with armour and clothing that is distincly Hellenistic in appearance, including strange Greek or Persian styles of helmets or caps with large feathered crests, or warriors from biblical scenes with swords that have pommels that are distinctly 9th-10th century 'English' in appearance. This confusing collision of equipment represented on sources of Dark Age visual evidence is a constant obstacle course for both historians and re-enactors.

Body Armour

Despite literary and visual references for a variety of types of body armour, there is little archaeological evidence for any form of armour other than ringmail being used by the Saxons. Apollinaris refers to 'studded deer skins' on Frankish warriors and there is a strong suggestion that shoulder clasps in the 7th century Sutton Hoo burial were fittings for a leather breast plate, but sadly, little organic material survived in Sutton Hoo, due to the extreme sandiness and acidity of the soil.

As far as scale armour is concerned, there are depictions on Saxon and Carolingian manuscripts that can be interpreted as scale plates but no archaeological data from graves or finds of a definite Germanic context back this up. The obvious 'classical'

Germanic style spatha.

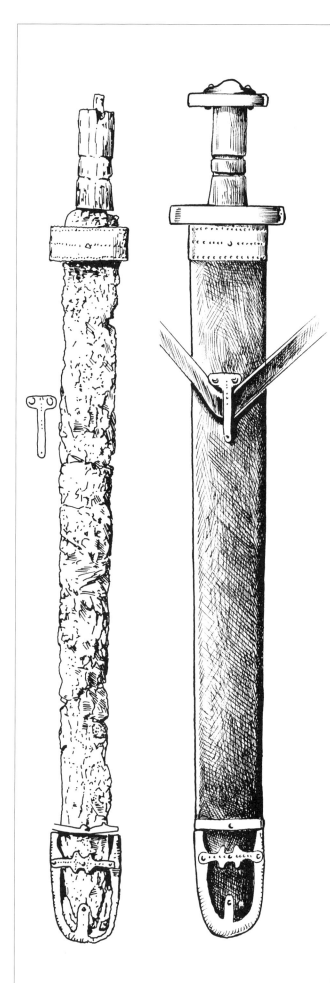

appearance of the equipment of warriors in certain English and continental manuscripts (pre 11thC.) suggest artistic invention rather than accurate portrayal of contemporary subjects. Some excellent examples of lamellar from Alamannic and Frankish graves confirm its use by Germanic warriors on the continent in the earlier part of this period, but no such parallels of a definite Saxon context were to be found in Britain.

Ringmail seems to be the most commonly represented type of armour in literary and visual evidence throughout the Saxon era. The mailed warriors on the 7th century Franks' casket carvings, various manuscript illustrations and of course the Saxon *huscarls* depicted on the Bayeux Tapestry suggest its use throughout the Saxon era. The life expectancy of a well maintained mailshirt could be generations even centuries; a passage from *Beowulf* hints at the bequest of a mailshirt (already of great antiquity) to a relative should the hero meet his end in battle: 'For it is the best corselet in the world, the work of Weland Smith, and an heirloom that once belonged to my grandfather Hrethel'.

Evidence for the continuing value of mailshirts can be seen on the Bayeux Tapestry as bodies are often shown being unceremoniously stripped of their mailshirts. The fragmentary finds of mail of this era are mostly Danish (Thorsberg and Vimose 300-500A.D.), Swedish (Vendel & Valsgärde helmet aventails 500-650A.D.) and Norwegian (Sodermanland, Splevik 600-650 A.D.). All are made from iron links in rows that are alternately riveted or butted – the Roman method of manufacture, at least, suggesting an influence here. The link diameters and wire thicknesses seem to vary from example to example, for instance, Vendel grave XI(b) has 6.4-7.6mm links made from 1.0mm wire, whereas Vendel grave I has the remains of a mailshirt made from 13.5mm links of 2.5mm wire.

A Saxon mail example found in Britain and well worth mentioning for that reason is the Coppergate helmet's aventail (mid-late 8thc. Northumbrian). This neckguard, when found, was in a remarkable state of preservation for its age and was composed of 1.1mm thick iron links that were 7.9mm in diameter and secured with tiny iron rivets. As has already been discussed (see Arthurian chapter), re-enactors fall back on a variety of material sources for mail manufacture, the most common being dark-finished square-sectioned spring-washers, which by a useful coincidence are often sold in the diameters and

(a) The Feltwell sword and (b) author's reconstruction drawing.

The Franks casket. This shows what appears to be a mailed warrior and a bowman.

thicknesses that would be acceptable for reconstructing aventails and mailshirts of this period. The most commonly used type are the (black-finish) 8.0mm diameter, 1mm thick washers; these proportions match the size found on the only surviving example of a full Saxon mailshirt, found in the7th century Sutton Hoo ship burial. This mailshirt's links had been alternately riveted or butted and, unusually, the rivets were made of copper alloy. When found, it had corroded into a solid lump of rings too dense for accurate X-ray assessment, but its mass, when compared with modern reconstructions, would suggest a thigh-length coat of mail.

Swords

There are plenty of archaeological and artistic examples of swords surviving the various stages of the Saxon era, and these often mirror their continental counterparts, from the earliest Roman style *spathae* to the tapering blades of Harold's men as depicted on the Bayeux Tapestry. Rather than trying to assess the abundance of factual evidence for the many post-Roman and pre-Norman Conquest British and continental swords we have decided to concentrate on a few examples which highlight specific progressions in style and technology of sword production amongst the Saxons.

What is considered to be the earliest surviving sword of specific Germanic identity was found in the hypocaust of the *tepidarium* of the excavations of the Romano-British villa at Feltwell, Norfolk (*Settlement, Religion & Industry on the Roman Fen-Edge, Norfolk Excavations* by Ernest Greenfeld, 1962-64. Sword comparanda and dating by Sonia Chadwick Hawkes). This has been dated to the first quarter of the 5th century and unusually for its great age, this iron sword

has survived almost intact, together with its scabbard fittings, including its strap-holder. From its main features, which closely resemble those on the swords of south Scandinavian origin (homeland of the Angles), it is likely that this sword came from that area. Though this sword is not considered to be of the highest quality for its time, its features deserve closer scrutiny as they provide great insight into the weapons borne by the people who fought with or against the Romano-British.

The grip is made from red-deer antler and its

The Palace of Westminster sword. Dan Shadrake.

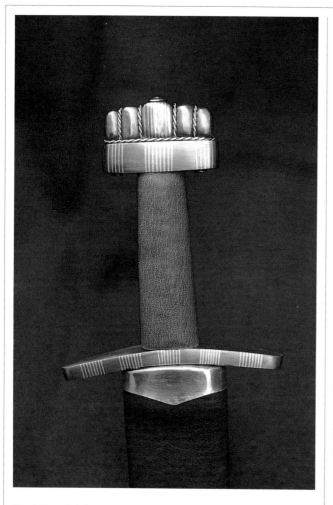

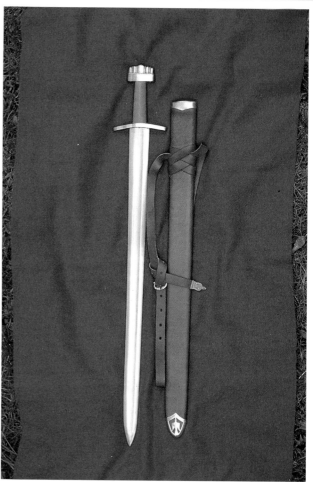

Top left and right.
Late 8th – early 9th century Saxon sword, the iron hilt features have been inlaid with wire and the pommel is divided into zones (Petersen classification type K). Reconstruction by Ivor Lawton of *Dawn of Time Crafts*.

Right.
Sword from the river Witham, 8th- 9th Century. *Sheffield City Museum.*

surviving copper alloy scabbard fittings are rather crude in their execution when compared to slightly later examples; an X-ray of the blade revealed that it was not constructed of the pattern-welded method. This example is at the earlier end of the 'Saxon spectrum' and overall quality of workmanship coupled with the strange nature of its hiding place (beneath the raised floor of what was then an unoccupied villa in the east of Britain) would indicate that it was not obviously the property of a rich man; normally Germanic goods would be found in graves together with goods indicating the wealth of the deceased, but in this case there is no way of knowing the rank or status, let alone the cultural origin of the sword's last owner.

During the earlier Roman years, the fact that

swords were regular army issue took away to some extent their role as indicators of social status. With the breakdown and dissolution of Roman *mores* and organisation, this role returned as well-made swords once again became expensive, hard to come by, and consequently almost exclusively the weapons of the warrior elite, whether Saxon or British. Fine examples of how closely the Germanic and later Roman military cultures were interwoven are the extensive continental finds of Nydam bog (mid 4th century A.D.) and Vimose (late 4th early 5th century A.D.) in which large numbers of double edged Germanic and Roman swords of varying designs were found alongside single edged war knives, spears, bows, mailshirts, shields and a host of other items both precious and useful. The lesson of these ritualistic burial hoards is that they were composed of such a mixture of types of swords that it is often inadvisable to apply our 20th century perceptions of military ordnance and cultural identity to ancient armies, however standardised they may now appear. However, with that proviso Nydam and Vimose along with the Feltwell sword provide quite excellent reference for migration era (early Saxon) sword reconstruction as there is every reason to

suppose that weapons like those found at Nydam and Vimose found their way to British shores along with their contemporary at Feltwell.

The Feltwell hilt seems to have been composed of mostly organic materials, as many early Germanic examples were; the Cumberland hilt (5th-7th century) has a wooden hilt, grip and pommel, and is likely to have belonged to a higher quality blade (considering the fine workmanship of the gold mounts).

The Sutton Hoo sword (7th century) when excavated in 1938 was found with its scabbard, sword belt, and fittings, and widely considered to be the finest of its type, was likely to be the personal property of a 7th century Anglian king (although the absence of a body in the excavated tumulus has prompted much discussion on the nature of its interrment). An x-ray of the blade has revealed that it was made by the pattern-welded process. Pattern-welding was used on European swords from the 2nd century A.D. and fell out of use sometime in the 10th or 11th centuries A.D. when a better understanding of the tempering of ferrous metals improved blade quality and output of European armouries. There were many permutations and differing results from this complicated and

Witham sword reconstruction (note silver inlay). Made by Ivor Lawton of *Dawn of Time Crafts*.

The Gilling sword, reconstruction by Ivor Lawton, *Dawn of Time Crafts*.

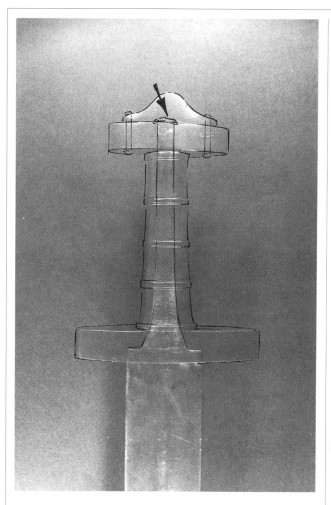

Inside view of an early Saxon hilt. The pommel cap's function is to protect and decorate the hammered-over tang (arrowed area). Robin Woosey & Dan Shadrake.

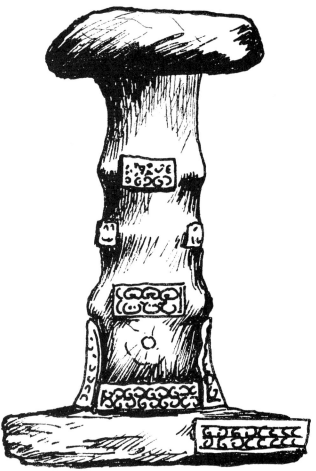

The Cumberland hilt. Dan Shadrake.

arduous process but the principle remains the same. A pattern-welded blade was produced by hammering a core of twisted bundles or strips of 'soft' iron between two 'hard' strips of high carbon steel. These hard strips were then forged to this core and hammered flat to produce a high quality, flexible and durable blade. The Sutton Hoo sword's blade core was made from eight bundles, each consisting of seven iron strips, the eight bundles were laid back to back in two rows of four, making the two sides of the blade. Each bundle of strips was turned either clockwise or anti-clockwise and laid alternately in the final arrangement; when hammered flat this produced a herringbone pattern on the blades surface.

There is strong evidence to suggest that this pattern was emphasised (often with either etching or a surrounding wire inlay to frame the pattern-welded area) as a boast of the blade's quality. There are several references in ancient texts to what could be the practice of pattern-welding. In this excerpt from *Beowulf* the hero says, 'Let Unferth have the blade I inherited – he is a widely known man- this wave patterned sword of rare hardness.' The Sutton Hoo sword's grip was made of wood decorated with two fine gold filigree clips that were similar in style to the Cumberland sword grip mounts. This oval section wooden grip was held between the pommel and hand guard which were themselves made from a metal core (possibly iron and now decayed) covered with sheet gold. The pommel cap served a function in that it was used to cover the worked or gripping end of the blade tang; it is of the 'cocked hat' type and had a copper alloy core on which five of gold and cloisonné garnet panels of the finest workmanship were fitted.

This richly decorated pommel cap matched two gold and cloisonné garnet buttons which were mounted on the scabbard and were thought to have been part of an integrally mounted double strap for fastening the waist belt to the scabbard. The scabbard itself was made of wood which was covered on the outside in leather and had an inner lining of wool; the natural oil, lanolin, present in the wool, would have acted like a protective lubricant. Obviously such a successful idea, this same principle of scabbard lining was present in some surviving scabbards from the later Viking era.

A fairly common feature on pommels of early Saxon swords is the pommel-mounted sword ring. The exact significance of these sword rings is not known, although it has been suggested that they were indications of bonds or contracts to a chief or even of religious significance attached to some long forgotten ritual. It is impossible to say what the exact reason for the sword rings' presence on pommels actually was, but many examples have been found across northern Europe and Britain.

The Palace of Westminster sword was discovered in 1948. Whilst nothing was found in the proximity of the sword to suggest a date, comparisons with continental examples suggest late 8th century A.D. *(The Palace of Westminster sword* by G.C. Dunning and Vera I. Evison).The Westminster sword blade was already broken when found but its blade was reckoned to be 74.6cm long and 4cm wide with a pattern-welded core that is 1.5 cm wide. The grip and pommel are lost but the cross-guard suggests a style similar to contemporary Scandinavian swords classified by J. Petersen in 1919 (see Viking chapter). The crossguard is iron and an obtuse oval in section; it is inlaid with copper alloy panels that have had a leaf scroll pattern chiselled into them. Sections of this cross-guard are inlaid with thin copper alloy strips, which were not intended to be the original form of decoration but have been revealed by a process of wearing away of the copper-alloy. The practice of inlaying precious metals and alloys onto weapons was common amongst the Saxons, Vikings and indeed most of the central and northern European peoples at this time, and the common technique of application was normally to incise parallel grooves into an area and hammer in the strips of alloy, silver or gold wires of a slightly larger gauge so that the wires' excess would spread out over the surface of the decorated hilt or pommel and merge to form a flat and featureless sheet on which a decoration could then be stamped or carved.

The pattern welding process. Dan Shadrake.

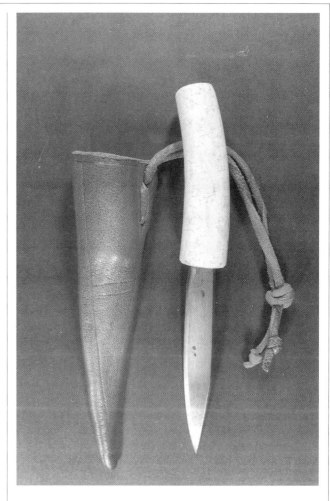

Bone handled utilitarian knife. It has a sharp blade for use in living history scenarios. Reconstruction by Ivor and Simone Lawton of *Dawn of Time Crafts*.

In this case the decorated surface sheet has worn away, leaving the anchor grooves still full of the decorative substance, which gives the sword the appearance of being decorated with inlaid wire, rather like fine plaster falling off a wall and leaving the bricks exposed. Surrounding the surviving copper alloy panels are traces of a black paste composed of calcium carbonate and iron carbonate; this paste was often used to decorate the hilt, apparently by adding contrast to the then shiny alloy panels. An abundance

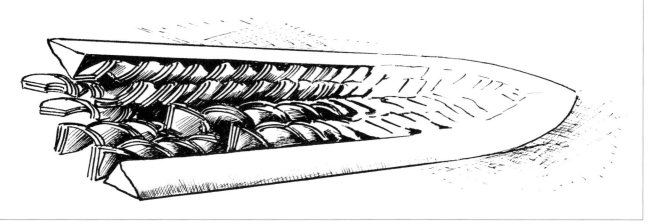

The Battle of Dunnichen (Necthansmere), May 20th, 685 A.D. Northumbrian Saxons against Picts.

The Picts under King Bruide were to accomplish an outright victory against the Northumbrians under king Ecgfrith at Dunnichen. The evidence suggests that the Picts employed a clever overall strategy in deciding the field of battle and in the execution of their battlefield tactics.

With the decline and collapse of the Gododdin, the Southern Scottish kingdom, in the beginning of the 7th century, the aggressive Northumbrian Saxon kingdom began to expand and take control of the former territories of the Gododdin and oppress the Britons of neighbouring Strathclyde and eventually the Picts themselves. Bede's account states that the Northumbrian king Oswiu, the father of king Ecgfrith, subjected 'the greater part of the Pictish race to the dominance of the English'. Following the death of Oswiu in 670 A.D. the Picts planned to rebel against their Northumbrian overlords, but news of the revolt reached the new king Ecgfrith who gathered a cavalry force together to crush the revolt and he did with ruthless efficiency, slaying a large number of Pictish rebels.

In the spring of 685, the Northumbrian army marched deep into the territory of the Picts and we have Bede's *Historica Ecclesiastica* as evidence that may suggest that the Picts were using a carefully orchestrated strategy of feigning flight to lure the Northumbrians to a battlesite that suited the Pictish style of warfare at the time.

Visual evidence for the arms, equipment and tactics of both the Picts and the Northumbrians is thought to be represented on the Aberlemno churchyard stone. We can only speculate as to the precise course of the battle, but the surviving evidence from sources such as the Irish Annals, Bede, The Anglo Saxon Chronicles and the stone Pictograms suggests that the armoured Northumbrian forces of mostly cavalry were defeated by lightly armed Pictish cavalry and infantry. The infantry seem to be arranged into a pike-block or phalanx formation (the only effective infantry formation against cavalry).

The Northumbrian in this representation wears a basic pre-Coppergate style of helmet also represented on contemporary Saxon art of the time. The neck guard of this helmet is depicted as solid rather than mail and the finish is an undecorated but polished iron. He also wears a mailshirt, carries a small buckler and a long stabbing spear; we can only guess at his horse harness, but have decided not to depict stirrups, as the representation of what could be Northumbrian cavalry on the Aberlemno stone isn't clear.

The Picts themselves are wearing long sleeved and knee length tunics, the question of Pictish helmets and armour in such early contexts has long been open to question, but despite obvious sources such as battlefield booty, no firm evidence of Pictish armour or helmets survive. Their clothing is chequered and not tartan (which came much later), examples of chequered wool fabric from the Roman era and later have been found in Northern Europe, England and Scotland; a good example of dark brown and light yellowy brown chequered fabric dated to the later Roman era was found in Falkirk.

Having no archaeological evidence for Pictish shields we have to consider the visual reference from sources such as the Birsay and Aberlemno stones; they are represented here as flat wooden circular and square shields edged with rawhide and painted with La Tène style patterns. The swords are based on the wide, parallel bladed, blunt ended examples also represented on Pictish art, although an example of a blade tip from the Argyll area may shed some light on blade construction. The simple La Tène designs on the skin of the Picts are tattoos, there is strong evidence from later Roman writers to suggest that the Picts marked their skin using this method but no evidence that body painting with woad continued into this era. *Painting by Richard Hook.*

of wooden fragments found with the blade with the grain running the blade length suggest a scabbard made of oak.

The source of the Westminster sword's manufacture was reckoned to have been the Rhineland, which was established as a huge centre of arms production in the later Dark Ages and the source of many Viking swords. This common source and the growing frequency of Viking raids in the 8th and 9th centuries had the inevitable result of cross-cultural pollination of weapons styles and methods of manufacture so that eventually there were to be only minor differences between the Saxon swords and those of their Scandinavian cousins.

An interesting development in swords of the late 8th and early 9th centuries was the variety of pommel guards. Some were divided into 3 or 5 section domes, of which the silver gilt pommel of Fetter lane is perhaps the finest example, and illustrated a further development – the evolution of elongated crossguards that curved away from the hand grip on some examples. These hilts were mostly iron and design of the actual structure of the hilt elements seemed to be enjoying as much attention as the surface decoration; no longer were they just the sensibly-shaped straight-edged bearers of rich embellishment.

Many re-enactors indicate that later Saxon hilts, because of their larger hand-grips and wider cross-guards are a little easier to use, especially when parrying another weapon away; the cross-guard can also be used to block and trap an opponent's weapon. Again this practical experience of recreating history

The curious barbed headed spear on the Bayeux tapestry may be an attempt at portraying a Carolingian winged spear as held by this Huscarl. John Eagle.

serves as an excellent illustration of the evolution of weapons technology.

The Gilling sword (late 9th-early 10th centuries), discovered at Gilling, north Yorkshire in 1976, is perhaps the zenith of these principles. This type of sword was considered by Petersen *(De Norske Vikingesverd,* 1919) to be the 'typical Anglo-Saxon sword of the Viking period'. This falls into a group of swords classified as Petersen type L, whose common denominators are guards that curve away from the hand grips and trilobate (3 zoned) pommels. There are other British examples of this type albeit with slight variations, and a pommel of the same design was found in the river Seine at Paris. Although the Gilling sword is referred to as late Saxon, type L swords are not unknown in Viking graves, indicating the cultural exchange,whether by trade, theft or battlefield looting, of weapons and methods of production.

The Gilling sword's iron blade is 700mm long from the cross-guard to the point and tapers from a width of 5.2cm below the cross-guard. A pattern-welded central core can be seen in the blade's shallow fuller. The hilt of this sword consists of two plain iron guards that curve away from the handle; the lower guard is slightly larger and measures 86mm across. Bands of decorated silver once encircled a wooden grip (now decayed) and the middle strip shows damage that would be consistent with a blow from another weapon, which perhaps may have occurred at the time the sword was lost, as it was found in a river with no contemporary material, and only minor damage which is likely to indicate accidental loss and not ritual deposit. The trilobate pommel is set into the curve of the upper guard and has a silver band that follows the curve of the upper hilt guard which is decorated with panels featuring a typically Saxon repeating leaf pattern. The middle zone of the trilobate pommel is raised into a very pronounced cone shape. All 3 zones are separated by bands of inlaid silver which have been incised with a repeating pattern- subtle differences in the zones of the repeating pattern – suggest that this was cut into the inlay rather than stamped. The armourer Ivor Lawton of *Dawn of Time Crafts,* has successfully made replicas of the Gilling sword and others from Petersen's type L classification, and he employed both techniqes of incision and stamping on the inlaid silver. Worthy of comment is the considerable amount of silver used in the making of these sword hilts, another indication of how costly sword production must have been, and another example of how present day craftsmen can throw light on the circumstances of weapon manufacture.

As we have already discussed, there was a fair degree of cross-cultural influence in sword design and methods of production, so that by the 10th and 11th centuries Saxon, Viking, Norman and indeed Irish and Scottish swords (the latter being in no small measure due to the presence and influence of the Norsemen in the Celtic homelands) were, with a few notable exceptions, evolving at a similar pace and to similar overall patterns. This would explain why swords represented on the Bayeux Tapestry appear much the same in both the English and Norman armies.

The trilobate pommel and thick straight or curved cross-guard(Petersen types X,V andW) persisted in archaeological examples and manuscript representations, but these designs were gradually superceded by the classic 'broadsword' pattern in the late 11th to early 12th centuries.

The Seax (Single Edged Knives)
Archaeological examples of the *seax* occur across all the areas inhabited by Germanic peoples. The lengths and therefore practical uses of this type of weapon varied from that of small utility tools (of around 10-12cm) up to sword length (1000cm)blades. We have already seen examples of war knives as secondary weapons mentioned in contemporary British literature (*Y Gododdin*, see late Roman chapter). Saxon literature obviously has its fair share of references to warknives as this excerpt from *Beowulf* will testify: 'The king once more took command of his wits, caught up a stabbing-knife of the keenest battle-sharpness, that he carried in his harness'.

A classification of *seaxes* is given by R.E.M. Wheeler (Museum of London catalogue). The earliest type (I) is referred to as the Frankish type; this particular weapon has two curved edges, one blunt, and one sharp, which taper in a roughly symmetrical way to a sharp point. An example of the Frankish type was found with its copper alloy scabbard fittings and pommel cap at Ford in Wiltshire. The grip was made of organic material which has long since perished, and interestingly there is only an insignificant cross guard on this earlier example. In general, there would be no need for a parrying cross-guard on what would be a

Before the 8th century, English spears can be characterised by a split socket.

Spong Hill spear, note depression beaten into alternate sides in the cross section of the blade centre. Nick Nethercoat.

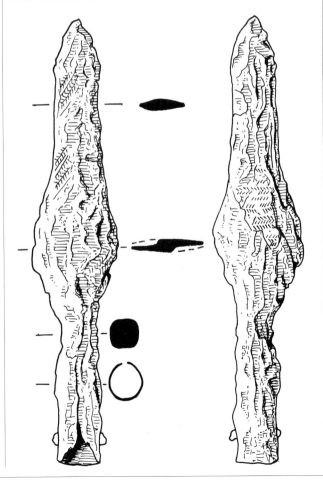

secondary thrusting weapon – the concept of knife duelling which owes more to Renaissance Europe, may have given rise to the development of daggers with elaborate quillions for this reason. Comparisons with continental examples have dated the Frankish (or Wheeler type I)to the 5th-6th centuries, and this type rarely exceeds 30cms.

The second area in Wheeler's classification, the type II, is referred to as the Norwegian type as finds of this type are quite common in Norway. They are dated to the 7th and 8th centuries and have a quite distinct straight back and curved cutting edge; an example from Norway was found with its hilt still intact. This hilt was almost identical to 8th century sword hilts classified by Petersen. The longest example of this Norwegian type *seax* measured 100.8 cms long and was found in a tumulus, along with a file, shield boss and three arrowheads. This type of *seax* was unadorned and rarely inlaid or decorated.

The Harbuck type (Wheeler type III, Fig 158) was found with a hoard of the same name and dated to around 900A.D.; a similar example was found in the Thames at Battersea, its blade decorated with copper alloy designs and runic letters. The Harbuck type was characterised by a straight cutting edge and a gently arched angular back, however the slightly later type IV or Honey Lane variety was a much shorter knife with

a straight cutting edge and a pronounced angularly arched back. A particularly fine example (found at Honey Lane, and from which the type derives its classification) is now in the British Museum and is inlaid with wire ornament. This was found with coins dated to the reign of Aethelred II (978-1016 A.D.).

The survival of single-edged knives in a utilitarian context amongst the military forces is without dispute, as such a practical, basic form of blade with the spine-like support of a blunt edge has enjoyed several reincarnations in later eras as a combined tool and weapon (Bowie knives, bayonets etc). It is likely that single-edged swords of this type persisted in use to the 11th century and possibly the 12th, but this is a rather obscure area, as lack of sufficient evidence of later single-edged types in warfare suggests their decline in or around the 11th century, and representations of double-edged sword blades on the Bayeux Tapestry are often too irregular or asymmetrical (due to the very medium of embroidery) to draw any conclusions.

Seaxes are well represented in early or late Saxon re-enactment and whereas smaller sharp utilitarian knives are confined to living history sections for safety

Re-enactment Seax, its point has been ground off by the armourer to lessen the chance of injury. Reconstruction by Pete Seymour. Lynne Smith.

Reconstructed francisca, *Milites Litoris Saxonici*.

reasons, battlefield examples are blunted and points are not sharp, but rounded to a safe radius. They are carried as a secondary weapon by spearmen, who often take great delight in using them in the confined crush of a re-enacted battle melée, where spears are rendered ineffective by the lack of space. Most *seaxes* are kept in leather sheaths that are suspended at an angle or horizontally from straps that hang from a waist belt, as indicated by grave finds, and later versions use handles of antler, bone or hardwood as metal handle fittings seem to be mostly confined to earlier versions.

Spears

The earliest Germanic spearheads found in Britain can be roughly dated to the migration era (4th -6th centuries). These examples owe a great deal to the Germanic adaptation of Roman weapons, indeed the long shanked *angon* was thought to be a Germanic development of the *pilum*. The later Roman writer Vegetius refers to this development of Roman technology of a previous era quite specifically: 'The javelins that the infantry army used were called "pila", having thin triangular iron heads 9 in. or 1ft long,

such as once lodged in a shield could not be broken off and, when thrown skilfully and with force, might easily pierce a cuirass. Weapons of this type are now rare with us, but barbarian shield bearing infantry use these particularly, calling them "bebrae", and carrying two or three each in battle.'

Vegetius refers to javelins as *spicula* and this clear indication that the *pila* were rare or had fallen out of use by his time, may mean that he is referring to the iron headed angons of the Germanic tribes. Like the *pila*, *angons* had a long iron shank with a tiny head (sometimes slightly barbed) in proportion to their body length and like *pila*, were throwing weapons. Recent tests with reconstructed *angons* by members of *Britannia* revealed how effective this weapon was; it was thrown at a target 25- 30 metres away and the penetrative ability was not in doubt after the head (2.5cms width at the barbs) punctured not only the uncovered wood of a 8mm plywood shield but also gouged the edge of a steel shield-boss flange on the way in.

A well preserved example of an *angon* was found in Abingdon in Berkshire (42cms long) and has been dated to the 5th century. The throwing spear continued in use through the Saxon period, for instance the 7th century Sutton Hoo burial yielded three *angons* and five conventional spears. Quite graphic reference to a throwing spear can be found in the ancient poem The *Battle of Maldon* referring to the Saxons defending Essex from the Danes in 991A.D.: 'Flashed a dart from a Danish hand, fist-driven, and flew too truly, bit the Earl, Aethelred's thane. There stood at his side a stripling warrior, young Wulfmaer, Wulfstan's son, fresh to the field. In a flash he plucked from its place the blood-black point, flung back the filed spear; again it flew. Home sank the the steel, stretched on the plain him who so late had pierced the Prince so grievously.

The Bayeux Tapestry depicts several instances of spears in flight; in one section where Duke William's forces 'fight against the inhabitants of Dinan', a plain type of javelin seems to be thrown by, and against cavalry forces. Spears are the most commonly found weapons in Saxon graves, and the associated find objects from all areas in the Saxon period indicate that their use across the social spectrum was universal. Only a few graves contain more than two spears (Sutton Hoo's five spears and three *angons*, or Yorkshire's Garton grave containing seven). Some early Saxon spearheads have a depression or corrugation beaten into them on alternate sides, this feature would have added strength to the wide blades on both these varieties. All Saxon spears are socketed and in most English examples before the late 8th century, the socket does not wrap completely around the wood leaving a characteristic 'split'.

The spearheads vary in design and manufacture throughout the Saxon period, continental influence played a major part in the development of Saxon spearheads so that by the end of the 9th century there were few differences between Saxon and continental examples of the Low Countries and Scandinavia. The barbed headed and ball socketed style of spearhead shown on the Bayeux Tapestry and contemporary manuscripts have no archaeological parallels in a late context and have been interpreted as artistic licence or stylized renditions of Carolingian 'winged' spear heads.

Axes

The small throwing axe or *francisca* was used by most Germanic peoples in the 4th-6th centuries, and there are plenty of British finds to confirm its use over here. The authors were fortunate enough to acquire an example found in Winchester; the head is iron and measures 12.5cm, the haft (of which nothing remains) was set at an obtuse angle. Reproductions show that hafts are not as effective when set at right angles or having haft lengths in excess of 30-35cm. The range of this weapon (20-30 metres) dictates its use at close quarters, probably thrown just before the moment that two opposing forces clashed. Throwing axes are referred to in the account of the battle of Hastings by William of Poitiers the Norman chronicler in his *Gesta Willelmi ducis Normannorum et regis Anglorum*: 'the English resisted valiantly...and they hurled back spears and javelins and weapons of all kinds together with axes and stones fastened to pieces of wood'.

The modern armourer Pete Butler managed to

Saxon axe-hammer, Sutton Hoo. Dan Shadrake.

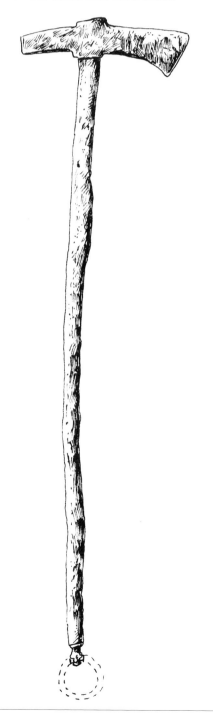

Francisca head found at Winchester. The two lines represent the original angle of the axe haft. Nick Ansell.

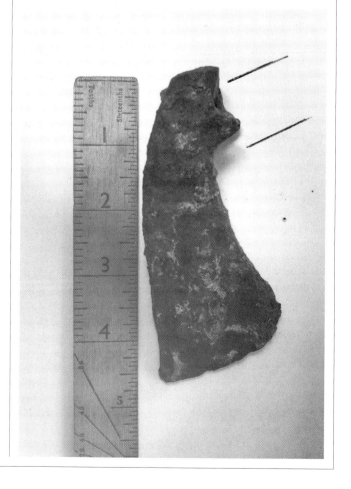

develop a safe but effective-looking heavy leather-headed *francisca* for use on the re-enactment battlefield, and the reaction of the audience when this type of 'throwing axe' is used is always a good indicator of how realistic it looks.

War axes amongst the earlier Germanic warriors were bound to have been used amongst the rank and file (the cost of swords would have meant that axes, as well as spears and basic clubs were carried by peasant levies)but were not just limited to the lower caste of warriors as the axe-hammer found in the Sutton Hoo tumulus indicates. Both the head and the shaft of this example were made of iron and it measures 78cms in total length; an interesting feature was a rounded component at the base of the iron shaft. An X-ray of this area indicates that it was likely to be a swivelling device for a carrying strap. The axe head extends backwards slightly to form a blunt hammerhead, and its appearance has been likened to contemporary and earlier tools but the length of shaft and associated grave goods make its use likely to have been for battle or at least martial ceremony.

Earlier Saxon axe heads are mostly functional and undecorated and quite modest in size and have far less emphasis in Anglo-Saxon poetry than swords or even spears. One of the finest examples of decoration on a Saxon era British axe head find was ironically Merovingian in origin (Howletts in Kent). The Saxon *huscarls* on the Bayeux Tapestry are shown wielding great war axes; from their representation on the tapestry they are likely to have been like the great Scandinavian style double-handed type, as Saxon weapons and armour were heavily influenced by continental fashions of the time (even the term *huscarl* is Scandinavian in origin).

Saxon axe-heads found in Britain. Nick Nethercoat.

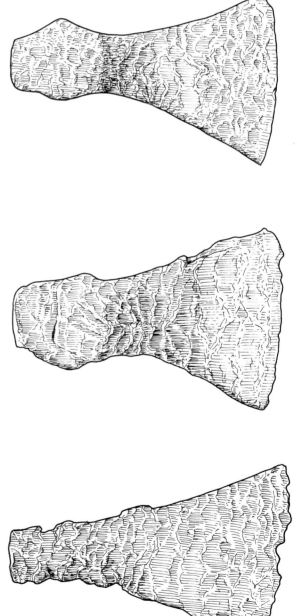

Saxon axe-head, likely to be the type used by Harold's Huscarls at the battle of Hastings. Nick Nethercoat.

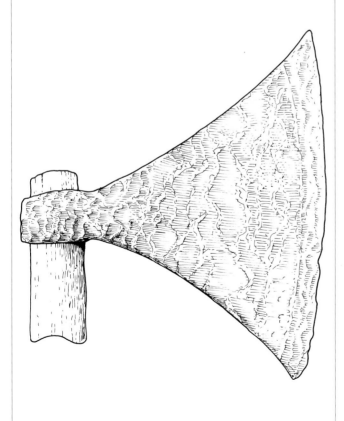

A succession of Germanic peoples were to push into the western Roman Empire in the 5th century. Here Goths and Franks are portrayed by *Britannia* and the *Swords of Pendragon* for *Corridors of Time* in Seventh Art's *The Huns.*
Julia Wilkie, Seventh Art Productions.

Shields

Despite the fact that almost a quarter of the graves of early Saxon males contain the remains of shields, no complete examples survive from Britain's Saxon period. Shield bosses survive in abundance but unlike later Viking age continental bog deposits (Gokstag) the surviving examples of board wood are at best, fragmentary and scarce. The size and shape of the total shields area (in English examples) can only be guessed at using a mixture of archaeological data and surviving pictorial images.

Concentrating on the pictorial evidence for the early part of this era, images on the 7th-8th century Franks casket panels and Repton stone indicate medium-sized shields with a roughly estimated diameter of 35-60 cm (14 inches-2 feet). The Franks' casket shields appear to be convex and there is no clear indication of how they are gripped; the later Saxon manuscripts and the Bayeux Tapestry show both flat and convex shields of a larger diameter estimated at a maximum of 107cm (3.5 feet). Later Saxon representations also show the kite shield being used by Saxon warriors, and this is thought to be yet another indication of how ready Saxon military society was to adopt the latest developments and fashions of continental warfare; sadly no archaeological data on Saxon kite shields of this era survives to the present day. Archaeological evidence for the wooden parts of early and late Saxon period round shields is rather scarce in Britain, and all shield fittings indicate their use on nothing other than round shields; the evidence for shield diameters are mostly gained from soil stains, although this is not thought to be reliable, as decomposition of the wood and metal fittings result in materials leeching into the soil in irregular shapes. Thanks to the survival of the gilded copper alloy edging (an unusual component on shields of this era), the Sutton Hoo shield's diameter was estimated at 91.5cm – scraps of limewood were found along with leather, which would indicate a leather cover. Re-enactors have discovered that a rawhide or treated leather shield front can greatly prolong a shield's life on the battlefield as the shock of blows is absorbed by this method of covering. Evidence for leather covering was also found in graves of lower status warriors, and in an inhumation at the Saxon burial site at Spong Hill in Norfolk a Saxon disc-topped boss, 5th-7th century, was found with part of its wooden board intact and fragments of leather between the iron boss and the remaining wood.

Styles and methods of boss construction varied throughout the early and middle Saxon era in Britain. A classification was proposed by Tania Dickinson and Heinrich Harke. Concentrating on 117 bosses from the Upper Thames reigion, they were able to break down the variants into categories. All the bosses shared the characteristics of being made from separate iron components, a cone, a wall, and a flange. The earliest types were modest in size (65-91mms high) and had straight sided or concave cones and four rivets connecting the flange to the wood (precise dating is obviously impossible but similar continental examples have been dated to 400A.D.). Later developments and permutations included five rivets fixing the flange to the wood, the application of offensive spikes or studs to the outside of the cone apex and larger more convex domes. The latter development was taken to extremes with the Lowbury Hill example; this type is dated from 650- 750 A.D. and whilst the flange and wall are

Saxon boss (c. 6th Century), from Spong Hill, note the offensive studs on the apex of the domes. Norfolk Museums Service.

conventional (some examples consist of only flange and dome), the dome has been beaten out into a long convex conical 150mms high and is set on top with a small iron stud – this long style of shield boss is often referred to as the 'sugar loaf' style. There are less variations in shield grips as they serve only a practical purpose; most examples are little bigger than boss diameters and consist of a short flat strip of iron, pierced with two holes for rivets. Sometimes this strip was flanged at the sides and the flanges were bent around a wooden grip. Surviving data from early Saxon inhumations has the addition of a leather and fabric material bond around these iron grips; this has been explained as grip padding or even carrying straps.

When battle re-enactors take their shoulder-mounted shields off they often wind their carrying straps around their bosses to lessen the chance of tripping on the trailing leather or fabric ropes. It seems likely that shields consigned to the grave would have their carrying straps wound carefully around the grip. Longer grips (6th century onwards) were another development in Saxon shields; the central section that is gripped and falls within the diameter of the boss remains of the same thickness and design as the smaller grips but extensions run far along the shield's inner body and terminate in circles or divisions that are riveted to the wood. Slightly less than half the long

The Repton stone.

grips are curved, indicating their use on convex shields, although the Sutton Hoo grip is a long and highly decorated long grip that has no parallels. Most grips are iron but a notable exception is the copper alloy grip (Orpington, grave 25).

From grave evidence the woods used on Saxon shields in this era were oak, alder, willow, poplar, ash or lime (the yellow wood that Beowulf refers to *'lindenwood'*). Surviving fittings (such as the copper

Most examples of early grips are simple strips of iron, pierced for rivets. Dan Shadrake.

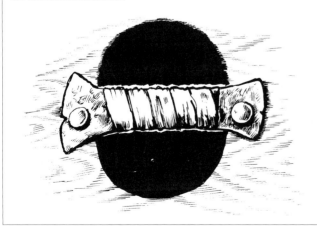

alloy fish fittings (Spong Hill grave 31), that were thought to be strap holders show that shield wood and facing material was an average of 1cm thick.

Belts

Early Germanic belt fittings are discussed in the late Roman chapter, although mid to late Saxon fittings indicate that belts were not as wide (no more than 3cm wide) and considerably less flamboyant than their early counterparts. From the 8th century, Saxon buckles were generally functional 'D' shapes that were fixed directly to the belt leather (not an articulate component on a metal plate). Less decoration was present on these later examples although strong Scandinavian influence is present on the more decorative examples. Copper alloy is the most popular material used although examples of silver and bone buckles are known. Later Saxon strap hangings display some fine workmanship. Carolingian and Byzantine buckles have been found in some Kentish graves.

Boots

Not much archaeological evidence exists for early and late Saxon shoes although the evidence there is suggests that late Saxon footwear was more or less the same as Scandinavian examples; early Saxon re-enactors (using the principles of equipment applied to *foederati* or *laeti* to source their groups) tend to fall back on basic designs of Roman footwear.

Brooches

The earliest Germanic/Saxon brooches in a British context were undoubtedly Roman in style but later developments and adaptations are varied, categorised into distinct groups and often used to date other artefacts of a more ambiguous nature found with them, because their distinctiveness makes dating and categorising easier. The few types listed below are very simplified in both description and date (following the principle that brooches, like weapons, must have been occasionally bequeathed from one generation to the next). The crossbow brooch (4th-5th century) is often found in Alamannic and Frankish graves although a few individual finds indicate their use in Britain in the early Saxon era. The annular (5th-7th century, with later variants) is a fairly common find, and together with the saucer brooch (5th-7th century), the 'long' or cruciform brooch (6th-7th century) is confined to the early Saxon era. The disc brooch has been dated to the 8th-10th century, of which the finest examples are in the silver Pentney hoard. The penannular brooch (with many specific variants) seems to have been used from the 1st century to the 11th century A.D.

throughout northern Europe in the later Dark Ages. Strong continental influence can be present in any of the brooch types described; like belt fittings, the most popular material was copper alloy, but silver and sometimes gold were used. Earlier brooches were often inlaid with garnets, coloured glass or enamel; sometimes traces of organic material in areas or 'cells' of the brooch indicate ivory or even coral inlay.

A greater concentration of imported artefacts are present in Kent, as the collapse of Roman administration at the beginning of the 5th century did

Top.
Sugar-loaf boss, c. mid 7th- early 8th centuries A.D.

Bottom left.
Early Saxon boss, 5th century. The bosses dated to the earliest part of the Saxon era have four rivets on the flange and a shallow dome.

Bottom right.
Saxon boss, 6th-7th century. This boss is thought to have been a slightly later development, note the fifth rivet in the flange and the addition of an offensive stud or spike on the apex of the dome. The spiked type of boss is not permitted by many re-enactment societies, as it presents a risk.

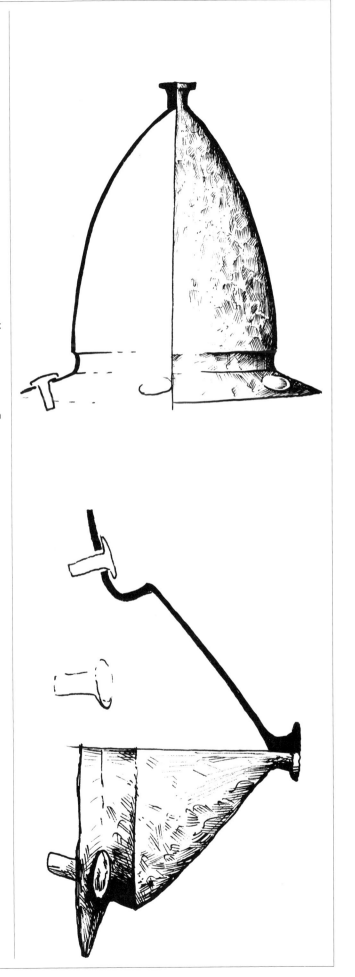

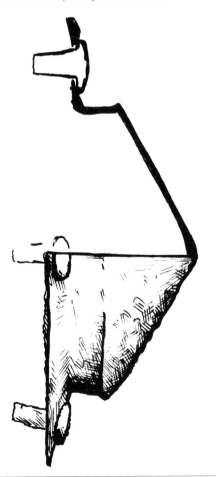

'Spong man', an early Saxon figure on a cremation pot lid, his head gear can be interpreted as a Pannonian or 'pill-box' hat; a style of headgear that was popular throughout the later Roman Empire. Norfolk museums service.

'Spong man' recreated, the author's interpretation of an early Saxon in a Pannonian hat. Stuart Klatcheff.

not bring about the end of trade with the continent, and Kent would have been the main recipient of goods (garnets from India, silks from the east) brought along an overland trade route from the Mediterranean via the Rhine valleys and the Alpine passes. Evidence for 'Coptic' bowls cast from copper-alloy are found all along this trade route but the heaviest concentration of this style of bowls is found in Kent. Strong Merovingian Frankish influences are present in Kentish grave artefacts at this time. Other evidence for trade with the Mediterranean in the early Saxon era is by sea. Leslie Alcock highlights the overwhelming evidence of 5th -7th century A.D. imports of Mediterranean pottery and glassware into the 'Celtic' west of Britain and the coast of Ireland that destroys the myth that the Saxons occupying the east of Britain had isolated the Romano-British and Irish from the outside world. If trade in domestic and utilitarian objects was possible with the Mediterranean so was the trade in arms. We have no archaeological evidence to support this fact; in fact the scarcity of

Romano-British finds in general has been explored in the late Roman chapter. A heavily laden Mediterranean merchant ship from this time was excavated in deep waters near the island of Yassi Ada, off the Turkish coast. This 21.3metre long clinker built ship (21metres long, 5 metres wide) was packed with oil lamps, tools and over 900 *amphorae* of wine. Enough of the hull survived to attempt a full-size reconstruction (now in Bodrum Museum); the interesting feature of a tiled firebox, mounted on a bed of broken tiles and pottery in what was a separate galley may indicate the fact that long voyages were taken, to the Black Sea, southern Gaul, Egypt or possibly even Britain.

Bows

Archers were certainly employed by both early and late Saxon armies; references in *Beowulf*, to a 'horn-tipped bow' shooting a man down, and later Saxon poetry including *The Battle of Maldon* indicates its use on the battlefield. The Franks' casket clearly shows an archer dropping a volley of arrows onto warriors with raised shields. The Franks' casket archer, and indeed the only English archer depicted on the Bayeux Tapestry both have bows which are represented as almost their own height, suggesting the possible forerunners of the English longbow. No British bows that can be identified as Saxon survive; the Nydam bog examples are surviving continental Germanic bows that have been dated to the migration era, and these are slightly shorter than surviving medieval longbows and were made of 'D' section yew. Unlike medieval bowmen, the Saxon archers seemed not to have been used as a decisive element in battle.

Cavalry Warfare

Cavalry or naval forces are aspects of warfare not normally associated with the Saxons. Since they are both subjects of misconceptions, we propose to discuss them together. Indeed there is poetic evidence at least to show that the Saxons, like their Scandinavian cousins, regarded ships rather as sea-borne horses, for

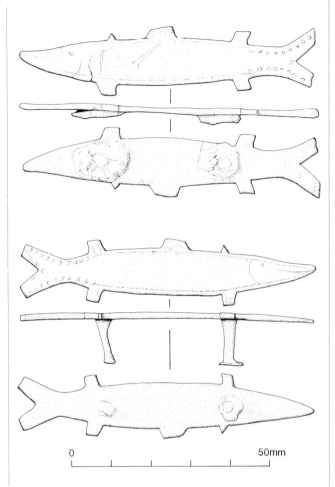

Right.

Surviving fittings such as these examples of copper-alloy mounts (Spong Hill, Grave 31), indicate that shields of this era were at least 1cm thick. Iain Bell.

Bottom.

Cruciform brooch (Spong hill). Norfolk Museums Service.

example in their reference to 'wave-coursers' (*Beowulf*).

Coming first to cavalry, it is an oft repeated myth that the Saxons did not use cavalry. This is particularly so at Hastings yet the reason for the absence of cavalry at that most famous battle may in fact have had a lot to do with its successful deployment 20 days earlier at Stamford Bridge. We know that horses, used as cavalry rather than transport for infantry were involved at the battle of Stamford Bridge. As the 13th century Norse chronicler Snorri Sturluson tells us in his *Heimskriingla* 'The hard-fought battle was first loose and light, as long as the northmen kept their order of battle; for all the English rode hard against the northmen, they gave way immediately, as they could do nothing against them... Now when the northmen thought that they perceived the enemy were making but weak assaults, they set after them, and would drive them into flight; but when they had broken their shield rampart the Englishmen rode up from all sides, and threw arrows and spears on them.' Although Snorri Sturluson is writing about the battle sometime after the event we have no reason to doubt his word as it is consistent with the large number of horse shoes

Early Germanic buckle from Oudenberg, Netherlands. Iain Bell, after M.C. Bishop.

found at the site of the battle.

In addition the monk Florence of Worcester, a chronicler writing between 1124 and 1140 (but having access to earlier accounts) is very helpful in giving detailed reports of these times. For example he writes that in order to oppose his brother Tosti, Harold had called up a large cavalry force and a fleet. Several other references to English cavalry have been made by Florence and these include a report for 1054 A.D. concerning a campaign against Macbeth in Scotland, one for 1055 A.D. against the Welsh; here Florence does indicate that the English fought on horseback because they had been ordered to do so, although it was not their custom, and an engagement against the Welsh in 1063, when Harold took a small cavalry force to the Welsh borders at Hereford to fight Griffin of Wales. With paricular reference to the 1055 incident, it has often been suggested that Florence's comment about the fact that it was contrary to English custom to fight on horseback is indicative of an absence of a tradition of Saxon cavalry; in the same way does the Battle of Maldon convey an image of a fyrd solely composed of infantry. However Ann Hyland in her book the *Medieval Warhorse* argues convincingly that 'it is hardly surprising that hilly border territory was unsuitable for cavalry warfare'. This can be taken more as a judgement against the unsuitability of the

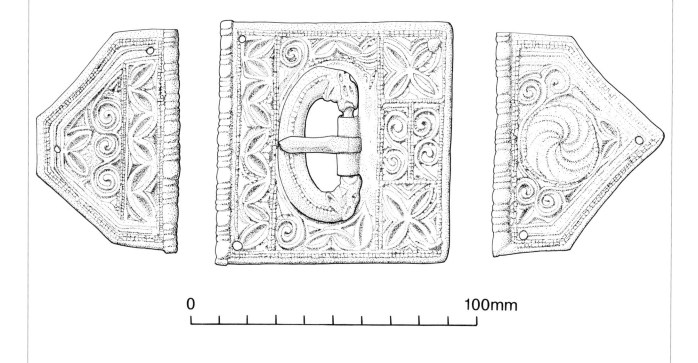

0   100mm

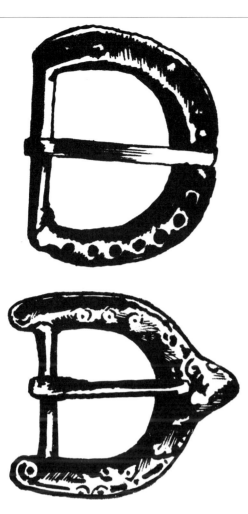

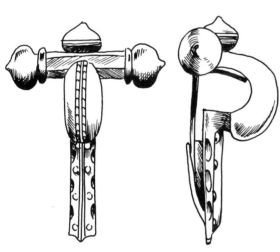

Top.
Later Saxon buckle, metal detector find. A.E. Mason.
Middle.
Scandinavian influence is present on later Saxon buckles.
Bottom.
Crossbow brooch.

Top.
Annular brooch.
Middle.
Saucer brooch.
Bottom.
Disc brooch, from the Pentney hoard.

terrain for mounted engagement rather than a Saxon disinclination to fight on horseback. The above accounts show that Saxon cavalry was by no means an unusual aspect of their military conduct. So, when Florence tells us that Harold, having waited throughout the summer of 1066 for Duke William to invade, then disbanded his forces when supplies ran out, we can safely assume that they included cavalry, since those same forces were recalled and sent north for the battle at Stamford Bridge. As we know, Harold

Recreated Early Saxon warriors at Sutton Hoo, featuring reconstructions by Ivor Lawton *Dawn of Time Crafts* and Ben Levick.

certainly deployed cavalry at Stamford Bridge.

Aside from Sturluson and Florence of Worcester, we have the indirect evidence of the chronicle of the abbey of Croyland and Anglo-Saxon wills which indicate that warhorses rather than transport or package animals were comparable in value to a full complement of arms and weapons; in fact in the lists of possessions over which the Crown had claim in the form of 'heriot', horses almost always are mentioned first, an indication of their military value. As for visual reference of Saxon horse warfare, there is the example of the eighth century relief carving of a cavalryman armed with a *seax* and small buckler.

Saxon ships are another obscure area, but here again we can point to a certain amount of evidence for marine technology throughout the Saxon era. The earliest Germanic vessels relevant to Britain were likely to have been similar to the example from the Nydam boat burial (Schleswig Holstein). This is a clinker built ship with a shallow draft but pronounced keel, it has oar rests but no evidence for a sail and the artefacts found on board put its date at around

Opposite.

Top.

After the 6th century, shield grips became longer and more elaborate. This grip is based on the Sutton Hoo shield grip. John Eagle.

Bottom.

The 7th Century Yassi Ada ship. Pro. George Bass Richard Schlect, *Archaeology Beneath the Sea*.

Some grips are flanged at the middle, these flanges are bent around a wooden grip. Dan Shadrake.

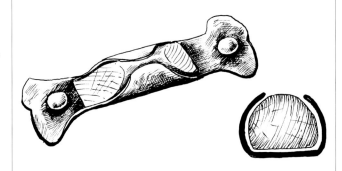

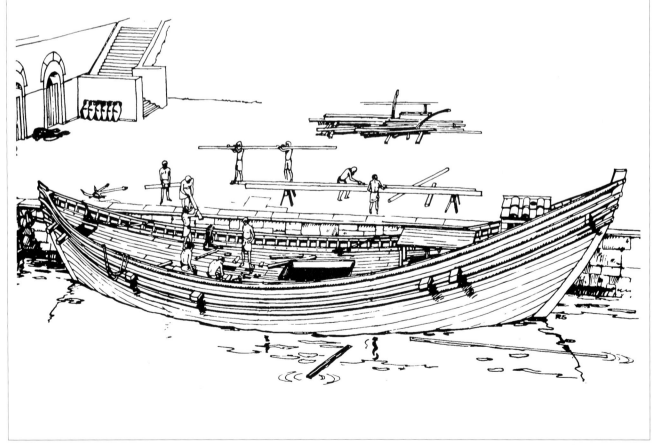

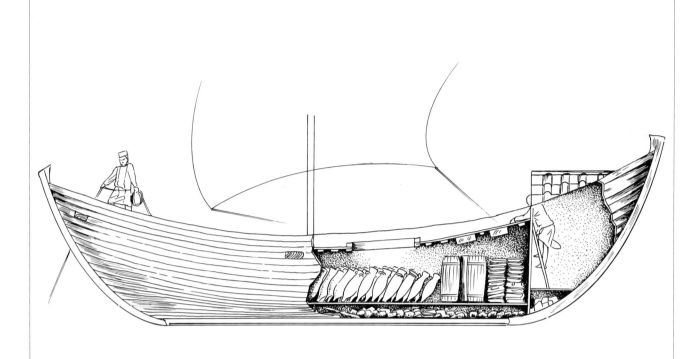

Above.

The remains of a galley and tiled hearth on the Yassi Ada ship may indicate that it undertook long journeys. Dan Shadrake.

Right.

The Yassi Ada ship was packed with oil lamps, tools and over 900 amphorae of wine. Dan Shadrake.

400A.D. The Sutton Hoo tumulus provides us with slightly later evidence for Saxon boat construction; although the structure of this 7th century ship had decayed long before its excavation in 1939, a negative cast impression was left in the soil indicating a clinker built ship of massive proportions (30 metres long), but again, as with the Nydam ship, evidence for a sail (in the form of a keel mount) is absent. Scandinavian ships were to undergo significant developments in the 8th century, in terms of sail and mast sizes; for a time this gave these Viking raiders technical superiority in marine warfare over their opponents (these aspects will be discussed in the Vikings chapter). However, this technology was to be adopted and improved upon by the Saxons under Alfred.

Vikings

It has so far been the business of this book to discuss cultures in terms of their military technology and its modern replication. However, it may be appropriate in this context to highlight popular misconceptions that have arisen about the Vikings. In many cases these have their roots in the passionately hostile records, mostly written by clerics who were the Vikings main prey and whose anguished prayer rose up from the churches and chapels of England: *A furore Normannorum libera nos, Domine* – 'from the fury of the Northmen deliver us, o Lord'. This jaundiced view was not limited to England; as the French monk Abbo put it: 'The wild beasts go through hills and fields killing babies, children, young men, old men, fathers, sons and mothers. They overthrow, they destroy, they ravage; sinister cohort, fatal phalanx, cruel host.' This was the damning judgement expressed throughout the whole of Christian Europe about the Viking raids.

A more dispassionate yet just as scathing view is expressed by an Arab merchant called Ibn Fadlan who came across them in the great market places of Europe and Scandinavia. He wrote contemptuously that they were the filthiest of God's creatures who did not wash after discharging their natural functions; nor did they wash their hands after meals. As a final insult he likened them to stray donkeys. So it is not surprising that the Vikings received what could now be termed a universal bad press. Yet they were also farmers, craftsmen and excellent traders who were responsible for establishing trading posts throughout an incredibly large geographical area from North America to Russia and from as far north as Greenland and Iceland to the most southerly outposts of the Eastern Mediterranean.

In order to understand what the Vikings' achievements were, and hence to describe their world, it is important to consider their origins. The Vikings were called by many names. They were referred to as Danes, Northmen, pagans and heathens, but the word Viking, itself, came to be used most often to describe not just the raiders themselves but their exploits over the three hundred years that they made such an impact on European history. It is not surprising that this three hundred year-odd span is often known as the Viking Age.

To be a Viking was not to possess a a specific nationality; Scandinavia, the lands of the Baltic, and the outlying islands were all homelands for Vikings. They may now be the countries of Denmark, Sweden, Norway, but to the Viking they were never single nations (in the modern sense) with separate identities. For this book, we shall use the term Viking to denote any raider, merchant, explorer or adventurer coming from Scandinavia or the Baltic area. The word Viking has obscure beginnings; in old Icelandic the word 'vik' meant a bay or creek, and perhaps it may have lent its name to the raiders who used those same creeks. Furthermore, there is an old Icelandic verb 'vikya' which means to turn aside and this may have been applied to the wandering raiders and explorers in the sense that they had turned away from their homesteads. More specifically, the Icelandic sagas use the word 'vikingr' as a word for a pirate or a raider; 'viking' means the expedition itself. So the adventurers went 'a-viking'; the stay-at-home Scandinavians did not merit the epithet 'viking'.

The Anglo-Saxon Chronicle refers to 'wicings' in several places and on each occasion it is used to denote a small band of marauders not an organised military invasion force. Only now in the twentieth century has the word Viking become the standard word in use for all such Scandinavian raiders and pirates. Western European commentators of the time used the term 'Dani' and 'Nordmanni' indiscriminately to refer to Vikings regardless of their homeland. It is as well to bear in mind that nationality had no meaning until much later in the Viking age when some of the Scandinavian states first established themselves. In this, the Vikings were not unique; after all, the English did not think of themselves as such until 973 when Edgar (Alfred's grandson) was crowned and received

102 Vikings

Reconstruction of Viking battle with members of *The Vikings* re-enactment society. The Vikings

the homage of the Welsh and Scottish kings and England became politically unified. As for the origin of the Vikings, this also is shrouded in mystery. The earliest known raids which could be described as Viking were perpetrated by the Southern Swedish Geats, a Germanic tribe who might reasonably be termed proto-Vikings. They attacked areas in the low countries of Northern Europe and it is likely that the warrior élite or at least the chieftains of the Geats wore military equipment similar to the examples known from the Vendel and Valsgärde graves. Since it is the purpose of this book to discuss and explore the original examples of equipment used by Vikings in their incursions and the difficulties in recreating and portraying the same then it follows that although the Vikings in their Scandinavian homelands were more than just warriors we will be concentrating only on the elements which helped them to achieve such great successes throughout Europe.

Opposite.

Southern Swedish Geat. These could be described as a Proto-Viking people (N.F.P.S- The Vikings). Jeff Johnson

Helmets

The Scandinavian sites of Valsgärde and Vendel have yielded striking finds, including a concentration of helmets in an excellent state of preservation. These helmets, despite varying in decoration and component style, all adhere to the same construction principles. All of the helmets found have prominent crests terminating in stylised animal heads at either end, and another characteristic common to the entire find is the decorative eyebrows which are based on bird or serpent forms curving over the eye spaces. These helmets possibly represent a bridging moment between the late Roman 'Ridge' helmet and the crested helms of the later Dark Ages. By their design, it is easy to see echoes of the later Roman headgear in the Vendel and Valsgärde helms, albeit that the latter is a more ornamented version, subject to the Germanic embellishment that has been discussed in the earlier chapter on the late Roman era. The dorsal ridge, wide brow band and rebated eyebrow areas of the Vendel examples are strongly reminiscent of the Burgh Castle and Berkasova examples of late Roman helmets. By the same token, the most interesting parallel as far as England is concerned is to be found in the Sutton Hoo burial of East Anglia. When images of the Vendel and Sutton Hoo helms are placed side

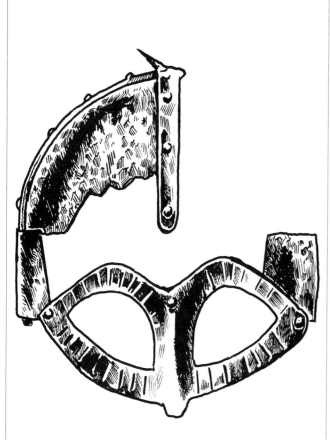

Gjermundbu helmet. Dan Shadrake.

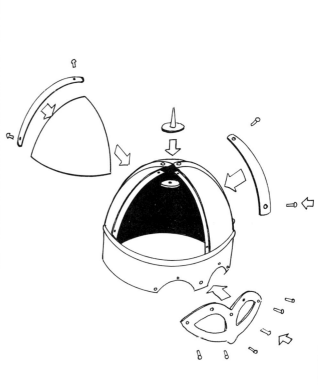

Anatomy of the Gjermundbu helmet. Dan Shadrake.

by side they share many distinctive features, particularly the richly embossed plates, which in both cases depict standing warriors, that a common manufacturer seems the most logical conclusion. Since popular opinion dictates that the Sutton Hoo helmet was likely to have been made in an English workshop and the source of the Vendel helm is unknown, such a conclusion, whilst inviting, is unsafe. In terms of its surface decoration, the Sutton Hoo helmet is most similar to the Valsgärde 7 with its gilded and stylised eyebrows and copper alloy decorative plates embossed with the same scenes. The armourer, Ivor Lawton of *Dawn of Time Crafts*, who specialises in reproducing equipment of this era, recently undertook a full reconstruction of the Vendel 7 helmet. An embossing stamp was manufactured solely for this project and the resulting copper alloy plates were tinned before being attached to the main body of the helmet. The result is a very striking piece of equipment which has the appearance of being made from precious metals, and indeed the original, in all probability would have been both silvered and tinned, particularly if it had been owned by a man of high standing. It has therefore been argued that such richly decorated examples of

headgear found in Vendel, Valsgärde and Sutton Hoo may have been limited to ceremonial occasions rather than the battlefield. The first recorded Viking raids on England were in 784 and 793 A.D. and it is likely that the equipment worn by these first raiders would have been less flamboyant than that of the Vendel culture for whose provenence only a Scandinavian origin has been specifically pinpointed. As for its counterpart in England, the Sutton Hoo helmet, it seems to have no English parallels and stands alone as an example of workmanship for which we can find no geographical neighbour.

The type of helmet likely to have been worn by the first Viking raiders to attack England is likely to have been much more functional and practical. Although it is an educated guess it seems obvious that the ceremonial helmets that have been discussed would not have been donned as a matter of course in situations that involved violent conflict and if they were worn at all, would have been limited to the chieftains and warrior élite in any raiding party. Despite an abundance of visual reference for the use of conical helms by the Vikings (for three such examples, see the tiny carved elk antler statuette from Sigtuna in

Sweden, the Isle of Lewis mounted chess figure and the relief carving of the Viking warrior on the Middleton cross at St. Andrew's church, Middleton, North Yorkshire).

We have no actual archaeological examples or even remains of conical helmets in a Viking context. In fact, the only evidence for such a helmet which can truly be termed Viking, in the sense that we are using it throughout this book, is the Gjermundbu helmet from Norway. This has some features which are similar to Vendel helmets in that the back of the neck is protected by a mail aventail and the face is protected by an iron spectacle piece. The method of construction, however, owes more to the *spangenhelm* than to the 'Ridge' helmets previously discussed. The *spangenhelm* comprises a frame of upright components linked together by segments of a domed or conical bowls. The Gjermundbu helmet comprises four external uprights riveted to four internal uprights and these in turn sandwich four segments, the segments are riveted to a brow band which also supports the spectacle component. This forms a particularly structurally sound dome because of the nature of the

Comparisons can be drawn between late Roman headgear and helmets from the Vendel and Valsgarde graves. Dan Shadrake.

distribution of the supports. The upright components are themselves thicker than the dome segments and therefore form reinforcing strips. The four uprights run from the front to the back of the head and from one ear over the skull to the other ear and meet at the pinnacle of the dome where they are sandwiched between two discs. The exterior disc has a distinct vertical spike which is just over an inch high; this has no reinforcing value and is considered by many to be an offensive element. This is a popular style of helmet with both later Viking and indeed Saxon re-enactors, as it has a definite archaeological basis and is comparatively easy to reconstruct. It is worth emphasising that in terms of re-enactment the spike is rarely left on due to its offensive purpose which must surely go some way to proving its original purpose as a weapon of assault.

Returning to conical helmets, the Lewis chesspiece previously mentioned is carved from walrus ivory and was thought to have been executed by an Scottish craftsmen and is believed to represent a mounted Viking conqueror. The question of Viking cavalry as apparently indicated by this chesspiece will be discussed later. The Lewis warrior is wearing what appears to be a single piece conical helmet fashioned from one piece of metal. There are two archeological comparisons contemporaneous with the Lewis piece

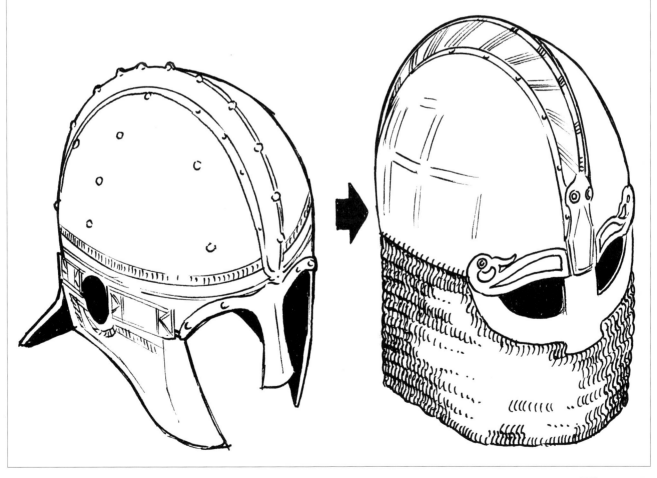

(a) Vendel grave 7, helmet front, (b) side & (c) back. Made by Ivor Lawton of *Dawn of Time Crafts*.

(itself placed between the tenth and the twelfth century), and these are the St. Wenceslas helmet in Prague cathedral and the Olmutz helmet in Austria.

The other interesting feature on the Lewis piece is what appears to be rounded cheek guards which are apparently suspended from a featureless browband. How much of this is influenced by the artist's limitations in carving ivory is not clear. However, the Sigtuna representation carved into an elk antler shows a pattern on the helmet which can easily be interpreted as rivets. The configuration of this pattern would suggest a four sectioned conical *spangenhelm*. Because of this overwhelming visual evidence many later Dark Age re-enactors of the Viking, Saxon and even Norman era use the four sectioned *spangenhelm* secure in the knowledge that despite having little archaeological provenance they can be used with confidence. Visual evidence for the aforementioned ridge helmets occurs less frequently towards the end of the Dark Ages and a safe assumption would be that they correspondingly fell into disuse compared to the conical helm. There would have been, however, a few exceptions and it is fruitless to speculate as to why the conical design won out over the ridge. Some have suggested the growing importance of cavalry as an effective fighting force in northern Europe would mean that the conical was a much more effective defence against downward blows from mounted assailants. Cultural distaste or the whims of military fashion cannot necessarily account for the disappearance of the 'Ridge' helmet.

Body Armour

We have little evidence for body armour worn by the Vikings. No complete mail shirts survive and what few remains there are, are fragmentary. The finds from Valsgärde and Vendel in Sweden are face guards and neckguards from helmets (circa 600-700 AD). These round or square section mail links vary between 4mm and 14mm in diameter and are made from wire which is between 1.6 and 2.9 mm in section. These are butt jointed and riveted in alternate rows using very small iron rivets, much the same as the Roman method of mail manufacture. References to mailshirts are to be found in both Viking and Anglo Saxon literature; the poem *Beowulf* refers to men swimming in mail armour, although this may just be poetic licence. There are later mentions of mailshirts in the Viking Age, for example, the Icelandic chronicler Snorri Sturluson implies that the lack of mailshirts amongst the Viking King Harald Hardrada's men led to their defeat by the English king Harold's forces at Stamford Bridge in 1066. Mail coifs are not well represented in sculpture and the iconography of Britain or Scandinavia, but the frequency of their representation on both the Norman and Saxon armies of the later Bayeux tapestry (as either separate items and integrally linked with mailshirts) would suggest that they are just another unremarkable stage in the evolutionary path of these items of kit. The lack of archaeological evidence for mail coifs in the Viking context has led to the unfortunate consequence that many later Dark Age societies are reluctant to use them before the era of Hastings when overwhelming visual representations cannot be denied.

The evidence for scale armour as used by the Vikings is rather flimsy and therefore unsatisfactorily as a basis for reconstruction. However, a couple of pieces of lamellar scale have been found in Birka in Sweden and it has been suggested that this may go some way towards confirming Eastern trade links at the very least, if not actually proving its use by Vikings in their homeland. Of course, the use of the segmented *spangenhelm* in itself already suggests a strong Eastern influence, and this is quite feasible considering the employment of Vikings as preferred recruits for the Varangian Guard, the personal bodyguard of the Byzantine emperors. Therefore it is not unreasonable to suppose that what was found to be practical and effective for the Varangian guard would have caught on once its efficacy became apparent to Vikings in their homelands.

Leather Armour and other Leather Work

The use of leather armour by Viking re-enactors is uncommon. The reasons for this can be summed up fairly simply. With Viking re-enactors as with late Roman re-enactors, the same dilemma presents itself, that no substantial archaeological remains support the application of full leather body armour in a Viking context, although there is a tantalizing reference by the thirteenth century Icelandic poet Snorri Sturluson to reindeer hide body armour given as a gift to King Olaf. We can only speculate as to the construction of such armour. In this we are assisted by some depicted evidence as there are certainly many representations of Viking warriors on tombstones, one of the clearest representations being the Gotland stone depicting scenes from the Viking afterlife. On this tombstone, a figure thought to be pointing the way to Valhalla to

Interpretation of the Lewis chesspiece helmet. Ivor Lawton *Dawn of Time Crafts*.

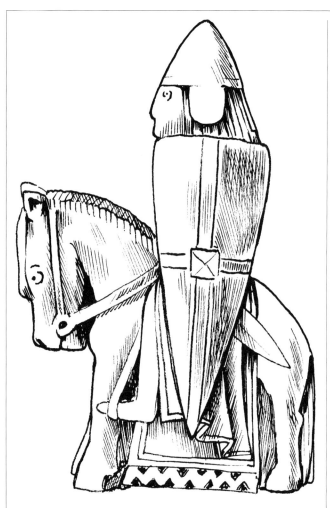

The Lewis chesspiece.

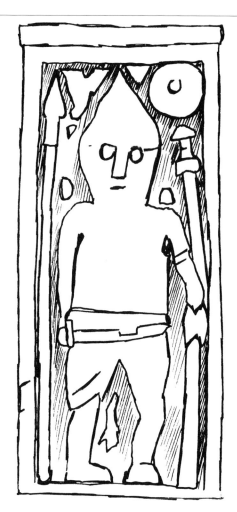

The Middleton Cross warrior.

two Viking mariners appears to be wearing a quilted jacket. However, what looks like quilted leather might equally be the interpretation of chain mail, scale or richly embroidered fabric. Unfortunately, there is no consistency or key which will tell us which material has been depicted; given that Sturluson records the gift of reindeer hide armour to King (Saint) Olaf it was at the very least a gift fit for kings and maybe not uncommon amongst warriors lower down in the ranking.

As in most ancient cultures nothing was ever wasted and by-products of meat consumption in all its forms were no exception. Types of hide which are known from literary sources to have been used include cow, goat, pig, reindeer, walrus, whale and other sea mammals, the latter two having particular importance as ship's cables and general purpose bindings. All of these types of hides were freely available, so it is no surprise that where plentiful evidence of meat eating is found in Viking settlements, solitary leather goods such as the occasional shoe or sheath have also been found. Because the process by which leather is obtained – the hides first separated from the carcasses and then cured – is an unpleasant and arduous one, it

tends to be situated in larger settlements where all the elements in the curing process are available in large quantities. By these we mean the curative and preservative agents which can be found in stale beer, urine, dog and horse dung, all of which are needed in copious amounts, hence larger settlements would supply that need.

A further ingredient in leather production is oak tannin, and again, to obtain this in large quantities, we would expect only larger settlements to have the wherewithal and the facilities firstly to convert and then to immerse enough hides to make it practical to do so. In the later Middle Ages, leather tanners prepared skins for sale onwards to leather workers who would then produce finished goods, but in the period under discussion we have no way of knowing whether or not this was the practice. Excavations at York in tenth and eleventh century buildings have revealed large amounts of waste leather left over from the manufacture of various leather goods which were obviously being produced almost, if not actually, on an industrial scale. However, despite George Benson's suggestion in 1902 that buildings between High Ousegate and Coppergate could be taken to be tan-pits lined with wood, these have recently been interpreted as little more than distinctive sunken building features; they are not now regarded as possible tan-pits.

Perhaps the most significant finds in the context of leather working are a wooden shoe last (21cm long) and many shoes in excellent states of preservation; the material used in most of the uppers was calf hide, as this is both durable and supple. The hide of mature cattle is more suited to sole leather, as it is very much thicker. The construction of these examples was mostly a simple enclosed buckled or button-fastened slip-on shoe. The Coppergate shoe (23cm long) was a particularly fine example of this type in terms of its state of preservation, and is perhaps for this reason the most commonly copied piece of footwear by re-enactment leatherworkers. The sole of this shoe is of one piece and is simply stitched to a two piece upper, which could then be easily replaced when worn out. Another very interesting example of footwear is yielded by the former Danish trading town of Hedeby (now inside the northern German border), and this piece is dated to around 950 AD. It is of a similar construction to the York shoes, but the significant

difference is in the height of the ankle area, which extends as high as the lower calf muscle, and the triple fastenings. The Hedeby shoe is considered by some to be the tallest example of Dark Age footwear.

Other interesting leather finds at Hedeby include two sling cups; these are slightly oval in shape and have a series of lengthways slits cut through the material. Drawing on the authors' own experience of using a sling, it can be tentatively suggested that the slits would have served the purpose of slightly opening around the pressure of the stone or baked clay missile, thereby holding it securely in place prior to release. When using a flat or slightly cupped uncut pouch even the most experienced slinger has to endure the frustration of an irregularly-shaped missile flying astray or dropping out altogether. Recent experiments using the 'cut' Hedeby style pouch seem to have almost eliminated such problems. Returning to the field of re-enactment, and as mentioned in the Late Roman Chapter, modern re-enactors use soft compounds such as mud or clay on the battlefield, and this type of sling pouch would certainly compensate for the irregularities of the modern, safer soft shot. Worthy of note is the opinion that specially selected

The Sigunta statue, believed to represent a 4-section conical helmet.

The Gotland stone, possible evidence for quilted body armour.
Dan Shadrake.

stones or missiles of baked clay are the most probable types of shot used as there is no archaeological, literary or pictorial evidence to support the case that Vikings used lead sling shot which seems to have fallen out of use towards the end of the Roman era. The Hedeby sling pouches have similar counterparts in York and Gloucester (dated to the 9th century and originally considered to be a hairslide), indicating that this was by no means an unusual weapon of the times.

Amongst the more richly decorated leather items at York are the fine examples of knife sheaths in which the complicated zoomorphic designs have been both embossed and worked by hand into the leather when wet; this is a technique still used by leather workers and an example from Parliament Street is likely to have been the sheath of a single edged warknife.

Belts of the Viking Age tended to be fairly narrow and an abundance of Norse belt buckles indicating that fact survive this era. Considering the Viking penchant for trade, it is not surprising that evidence for the wearing of these belts may well merely indicate use by other people of the time, such as the Saxons, rather than just Vikings. As already mentioned, the buckles of this time-period indicate that belt widths were rarely if ever over an inch wide. They are in many cases richly decorated but even so still fairly modest when compared to the wide and rather garish Germanic fashions of the 4th to 6th centuries. The most common material for buckles and brooches would have been copper alloy as it was both cheap and plentiful, but silver, also plentiful, was a more highly favoured metal for Viking art and currency and in fact silver was the metal preferred by Vikings as a form of currency both in coinage and in its own right. This liking for silver may well have provided enough motivation for many a raid on British and European monasteries, containing as they did ceremonial treasures which were most often made of silver and gold, such as crucifixes, pyxes and ciboria. Hundreds of Viking Age silver hoards have been found throughout Scandinavia and often consist of coins, brooches and rings. These hoards often contain a percentage of jewellery and coins which have been cut into small fragments in order that they may be used as the Viking equivalent of small change. This was called hacksilver and when enough was acquired it could be melted down into large ingots for trade purposes. Although silver held first place in the Viking's heart for both pragmatic and aesthetic reasons, gold had its place but was obviously more scarce and therefore was not as useful to the ever-practical Vikings. Additionally, gold thread was woven into clothing, and the Norwegian King Olaf Tryggvason in a spectacular

Later Viking warrior 9th-11th Century (The Vikings- N.F.P.S.).
Jeff Johnson.

display of opulence had the prow of his ship covered in gold leaf.

Shields
There are plenty of examples of shields of varying sizes represented in Viking art, but the only Norse examples that survive with intact wood are the shields from the Gokstag ship burial. The diameter of the finest example is 94 cm and is made of ash. The small hemispherical boss is slightly irregular but has an approximate diameter of 21 cm and a very small flange. The shields seem to have been painted in either black or yellow and may have alternated in colour down the side of the ship. No data has been made available on the pigments used on the Gokstag shield, but other surviving fragments indicate that in this case the paint was applied directly to the wood. However, this may not always have been the case, as there is an example of a shield with traces of painted leather covering wooden board in a burial pit at Ballatear on the Isle of Man. This latter shield is part of the grave goods of a first generation Viking settler, a young male of approximately 25 whose other

Recreated Viking warrior with spear and leather covered shield, *(The Vikings- N.F.P.S.).* Jeff Johnson.

The Norse film and Pageant Society represent Vikings using the most up to date archaeological data. Jeff Johnson

belongings placed with him included a deliberately broken sword which had then been replaced in its scabbard, and two broken spears. Therefore it is wiser not to assert only one particular type of shield construction as representative, as from the two examples just mentioned it is obvious that that the Vikings painted directly onto wood but also onto leather covering the shield, whichever was practical.

Returning to the Gokstag shields, the theory that they were made for burial ceremony and were never intended for battle since a protective covering of hide is absent, is not inconsistent with their location en masse in the context of a ship burial, as opposed to the solitary inhumation of the young Viking settler at Ballateare whose shield might just as easily have been used for battle as not, before finding its way into the grave. Some re-enactors consider Gokstag shield reconstructions a little too big and unwieldy. It is just as easy to speculate that such a functional and basic shield was designed to take the punishment of a battle. The wooden element, which has had very little time and effort put into it, as opposed to the boss, the grip and the edging, could be discarded with impunity.

Shields were invariably round until the late tenth century. At this time the kite shield seems to have appeared in Viking art in the late 10th century, and is thought to have been a development of an increasing emphasis on cavalry warfare, which would have demanded less unwieldy shields for mounted use. Certainly, by the time of the Norman Conquest they are widely represented in the art of the Vikings, Saxons and of course the Normans in the Bayeux tapestry, where round shields (and at least one oval) seem to have been the exception.

Swords

The sword in Viking culture was significantly more than just a weapon, having a religious aspect; after all, a warrior who died with a sword in his hand was guaranteed a place in Valhalla. The Norse poets and chroniclers of the Viking Age place great emphasis on this weapon, for example, names such as 'Odin's Flame' or the 'Wolf of the Wound' were given to swords, and reputations attributed to them as if they alone (and not the warriors who bore them into battle) were responsible for death dealing and mutilation. It is an interesting reflection of the Viking character that a people with such a strong emphasis on the deeds of the hero could be prepared to let the swords take the credit, at least in part, for the mayhem that inevitably followed Viking assaults.

The majority of swords from Viking Age Scandinavia have long, parallel-sided, double-edged blades which were mostly fullered to reduce weight and which tended to terminate in a rounded point, indicating their primary use as a slashing weapon (rather like the Celtic and later Roman *spathae*) as opposed to a thrusting one. Like those of the Saxons in the same era, single-edged swords are not uncommon in a Viking context. However, Scandinavian examples, the *langseaxes*, unlike their Saxon counterparts are very rarely inlaid with wire decoration. The long *seax* examples often compare in both length (up to 3ft) and hilt design to double-edged Viking swords. The majority of single-edged swords are dated to between the 7th and the late 8th centuries, although curved-backed *seaxes* are considerably less frequent in Scandinavian sites than their straight-backed contemporaries.

There are thousands of surviving examples of Viking Age swords across Europe, occurring in a variety of forms, and they are all grist to the re-enactor's mill. In 1919, J. Petersen published his study of Viking period swords found in Norway and his classification of sword types still stands as a point of reference for military historians and armourers. Petersen's earliest sword examples (types A and B), belong to the early part of the Viking age; these have distinct but rather modestly proportioned hilts, the cross guards being quite plain. These examples are very slightly reminiscent of the surviving Roman and Germanic *spathae* of the Nydam boat burial. By far the best illustration of the transition between the Germanic migration era and the Viking Age is an example found at Gotland in Sweden, whose hilt was metal and richly decorated with interwoven zoomorphic forms. Its overall shape has much in common with hilts of earlier Merovingian swords (these were often wooden hilts sandwiched between two plates of metal, a design which persisted into later eras when the entire hilt was to be made of metal). The largest category of Viking swords in Petersen's classification was the wide-hilted and triangular-pommeled type H and this is reckoned to have been in use between 800 and 950 A.D. One of the swords from Petersen's classification is the Steinsvik sword (belonging to special type I), which has an oval sectioned cross guard and pommel base, both of which having been inlaid with wire and embossed plates. This has an interesting English parallel in the sword example found at the Palace of Westminster in London and it has been speculated that, although unlikely to have found its way to London in a Viking raid because of the relatively early date attributed to this design (c. 700-800 A.D.), the swords may share a common geographical point of manufacture, possibly the Rhineland. This may serve as an indicator of how culturally similar the Vikings were to the Saxons in their weapons technology. To further this theory, Petersen states that although a large proportion of Viking Age swords were manufactured in Norway many were imported from Europe, the Rhineland being a major centre of sword manufacture at this time. It is not always possible to tell the sword's cultural origin since techniques of blade production differed little across northern and central Europe at this time; decorated components such as the hilt or surviving scabbard fittings can sometimes provide a good indication to the sword's place of manufacture.

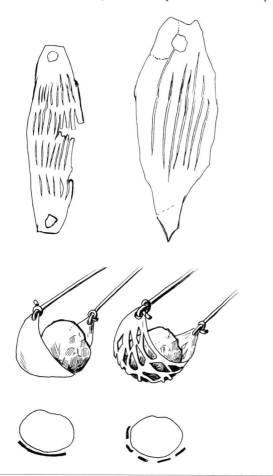

Top.

Sling cups from Hedeby. Dan Shadrake.

Left.

The slits on these sling cups may have opened slightly to grip the ammunition.

Top.
Gokstag shield. University Museum of National Antiquities Oslo, Norway.

Right.
Gotland sword.

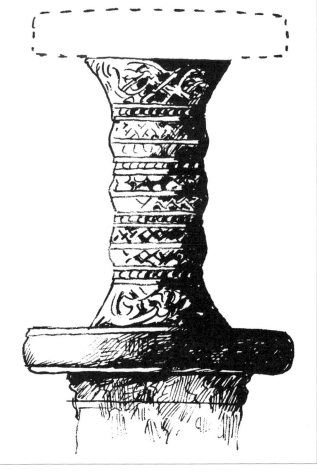

Surface decoration could include semi-precious gems like garnets (Petersen group 1a; Suffelweirhersheim sword, Strasbourg), which were very popular and hence very common. The Suffelweirhersheim sword is an excellent example of a richly decorated early Viking hilt; the proportions and overall shape of the pommel put it well into the Viking Age but again, the decoration is very Merovingian in appearance. This is typified by simplistic, stylized animal forms that have inlaid garnets for eyes, garnets also being used to cover the rivets holding the cross guard together. The simple swirling animal patterns are of inlaid brass wire. In fact, wire inlay using precious and other metals was commonly used for weapon decoration in the Viking era, and is a key aid to identifying Viking origin in a specific item. Often, large quantities of gold or silver were drawn into wire for this purpose. As mentioned in the Saxon chapter, the techniques for applying this to the sword hilt, axe-

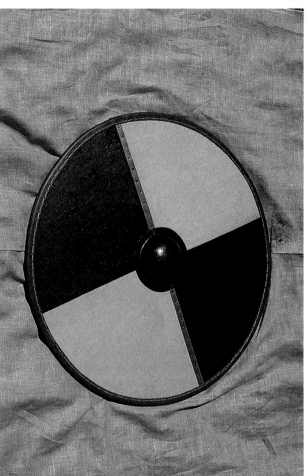

Reverse of a reconstructed Gokstag shield, made by Ivor and Simone Lawton of *Dawn of Time Crafts*.

Front of Gokstag shield replica, made by Ivor and Simone Lawton of *Dawn of Time Crafts*.

head or spear-shaft can vary, but the results are always impressive on both reconstructed weaponry and the surviving archaeological pieces themselves. We have already discussed the great importance of precious metals in Norse decorative art and weapon embellishment and this is evidenced by the contemporary literature of the Vikings as this passage from St Olaf's Saga will illustrate: 'There were in the house not a few gold ornamented swords. Sigvat made a stanza, in which he said he would accept a sword if it were given to him by the king. The king took one and gave it to him: the hilt was bound with gold, and the guards were gold ornamented: it was a very costly weapon.'

Many modern experiments have been conducted into the replication of Viking blades, and in this respect, the process of pattern welding presents the most challenges to the modern armourer. Pattern welding is the process of twisting and hammering rods of iron into a flexible but durable weapon and was thought to have been used before improved smelting technology was to produce consistent quality steel. It is a very labour-intensive way of producing a high

quality and high performance blade. Its use in arms manufacture ran from around the end of the 2nd to the 10th centuries A.D., and there is certainly no shortage of archaeological instances in Viking and Saxon blades. Pattern welding by its very nature often leaves a distinct, curiously interlocked or zig-zag pattern. References to pattern welding in literature of the time are not unknown, although infrequent, a famous instance being that of Beowulf's sword which is called 'graegmael' that is, grey patterned. Similar references are to be found in much later Scandinavian poetry.

The quality of blades could vary considerably, rather like the quality of car manufacture in the late 20th century and, like the motor car, the possession of a sword in this heroic age was often indicative of rank and status. Reference to testing blade quality can also be found in Svarfdaela.: 'Thorolf took his own sword and gave it to Thorstein; it was a fine and well-made sword. Thorstein took it, drew it, and catching its point, bent the blade between his hands so that the point touched the guard; he let it spring back, and it did not straighten again. He gave it back to Thorolf, and asked for a stronger weapon.'

Surviving Viking scabbards of this era indicate that they were made from wood covered in leather and in some cases lined with sheepskin; the lanolin in the sheep's wool may have provided a natural rust deterrent. A recent excavation at Skerne in Humberside revealed a sword still in its scabbard of willow poplar, the scabbard having been lined with fleece. It was found with four knives, some agricultural tools and a significant number of animal bones in the proximity of what appears to be the oak remains of a jetty or bridge. With the exception of one horse skull none of the bones show signs of damage associated with butchery for consumption. From this evidence one can easily assume that the Skerne site was likely to have been one of ritual deposit, not just butcher's waste disposal area.

Like the Celts and the early Saxons, the Vikings possessed a culture full of rituals associated with their weapons, and like the Celts, they often consigned their swords to the water in sacrificial gestures (or broke them deliberately. The exact significance and ceremonial functions of these ritual actions are lost to us but it is worth mentioning that over thirty Viking swords have been found in British rivers and a large percentage of these were from the Thames or its tributary rivers.

Finds of knives are very frequent at Viking sites in Britain and Europe, and the excavations at York have revealed hundreds of examples, mostly single edged small *seaxes* which were probably more for craft, hunting or everyday domestic use rather than combat, although the single-edged knife was an all purpose tool which could as easily be used in war as peace. Some Viking Age knives such as the example from 16-22 Coppergate (21cms in length) have revealed the tell-tale signs of pattern-welding, indicating that their intended use was for more than just light domestic functions, as a knife of such expensive manufacture would surely not have just been wasted on, for example, poultry trimming.

Many knives of the Viking era have been replicated for use in living history sections of various societies. Their effectiveness in specialist activities, such as leather working, hide cleaning, tanning, and preparation of foods appropriate to the era soon becomes apparent with use. Perhaps the most interesting knife to be copied by modern craftsmen is the folding knife found in Canterbury; this has a richly carved bone handle and the remains of two iron blades

Viking sword from the river Idle. Sheffield City Museum.

The 'high boot' from Hedeby. (c. 950 A.D.) Ivor Lawton.

Petersen's Type 'K'.

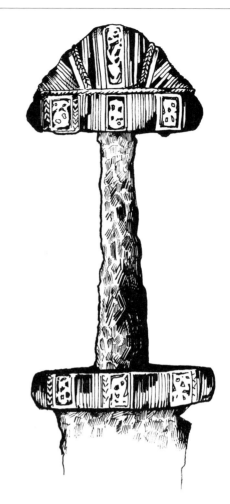

Steinsvik sword (Special type I).

Spears

Due to their simple design, ease of manufacture and frequency of finds, we cannot avoid the conclusion that the spear was the most common weapon of the ancient and indeed the medieval soldier. As we have discussed in the late Roman chapter, the spear could be used by both infantry and cavalry, low and high status warriors. In combat it was most effective in organised ranks and on open ground, a fact to which many modern re-enactors will testify. Viking spears occur in such a variety of shapes and sizes and despite there being less emphasis on this weapon in Norse art and poetry, spears are still found in sites where their presence can be interpreted as an indication of ritual deposits rather than chance losses. As with sword manufacture, Viking spearheads could be pattern-welded and decorated with wire inlay and gilding and the Vikings are known to have imported spearheads as they did swords as well as manufacturing their own.

It is arguable that some of the most distinctive imports and thereby influential on account of their special features were the Carolingian winged spear-heads; these broad-bladed weapons had two protrusions jutting out from either side of the socket. It has been suggested that the precise function of these protrusions is to prevent the spear from total penetration of its unfortunate target making retrieval easier. In one of these fortuitous developments which often follows distinctive styles of battle re-enactment, societies such as the *Norse Film and Pageant Society* (Vikings) and *Regia Anglorum* (Saxons) have found in certain battle scenarios that the winged Carolingian style spear can be used very effectively to hook an enemy's shield out of the tight, locked formation of the shield wall, thus exposing the unprotected body of the opponent long enough for another weapon to find its mark.

Most Scandinavian spearheads are socketed and would have been fixed to the shaft by single or double rivets. Such is the diversity of Viking spear-heads that specialist use would seem to be indicated for at least some of them. The smaller, narrower-headed spears are considered to be throwing spears, rather like the late Roman *spiculum* or the Germanic *angon*. An interesting description of the use of two spears at once

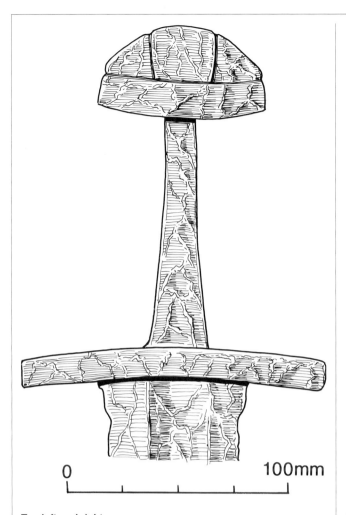
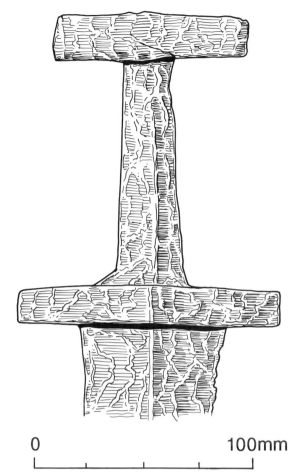

Top left and right.

Some of the swords from Petersen's classification of Viking blades. Iain Bell.

is to be found in an old Norse saga concerning a Christian warrior called Tryggvi who, when mocked by his opponents for being the son of a priest, threw a shower of spears at them with both hands and cried 'That is how my father taught me to say Mass!'

The Bow

Although it does not form part of the cliché Viking image, the bow was certainly used in Viking battles, and records of this occur frequently. One early Viking saga writer described the hail of arrows in a sea battle as 'making the sea look like it does in heavy rain during still weather'; the Norse poet Halldor Hermannson in his *Illuminated manuscripts of the Jonsbok* paints a vivid picture of a naval battle between Norway's King Olaf Tryggvason and some of his many adversaries including one of his nobles, the disaffected Earl Eirik who had joined forces with King Svein of Denmark and King Olaf of Sweden: 'And whistling arrows quickly flew Against the serpent's gallant few'. Indeed, East Anglia's King Edmund was martyred by a hail of Viking arrows, and a Church chronicler wrote some time afterwards that he resembled a sea urchin 'whose skin is closely set with quills'.

Unexpectedly for such a fragile organic item, many examples of Viking Age bows have been found; one such bow found in Ireland along with a Viking style sword was a 'D' section yew bow measuring 185cms. Numerous Viking arrowheads that have survived are mostly iron and either tanged or socketed; they can be broad-headed, leaf-shaped or barbed and examples can be anything up to 10 cms in length. Socketed arrowheads are more than likely to be hand forged than cast, and modern replications require a great deal of skill to produce. A double Viking grave containing six arrowheads along with a sword and a single-edged Saxon style knife was discovered in 1966 at Sonning in Berkshire. Whether a bow was buried with the arrows and if the arrows had significance in the afterlife as hunting or battle implements is not known.

Axes

No chapter on Viking arms and armour would be complete without discussing the war axes which are so popular and ubiquitous in the romantic literature of more recent times but which also have a strong basis in archaeological and literal fact. In many cases in Scandinavia and Britain, axe-heads seem to have been

Recreated Viking bowman *(The Vikings- N.F.P.S.)* Jeff Johnson.

this versatile tool other than warfare.

Ships

In military terms, one of the most obvious advantages the Vikings had over their contemporaries was in the area of marine technology. As we have discussed in the previous chapter, sea raids and actual colonization by the Germanic/Scandinavian peoples were perpetrated on numerous occasions before the benchmark raid on Lindisfarne in 793 A.D., which for many marks the start of the true Viking era. The practice of clinker building was known to many cultures prior to the Viking period and in fact Basil Brown's excavation of the Sutton Hoo ship burial in 1938 revealed that a staggering 29 metre length boat had been interred at that site some time in the late 6th century. The configuration of the surviving rivets and planks (of which only a negative cast remained in the poor soil surrounding it) revealed what could be interpreted as a double-prowed clinker-built vessel not unlike the ships of the Viking era which followed. Contemporaneously with Sutton Hoo, the Gredstedbro boat from Denmark revealed similar methods of construction.

However, at some point in the eighth century certain developments in Scandinavian warship manufacture were to add a vast dimension to both trade and military conquests of the far travelling Norseman, a marker for the unfurling of the Viking Age upon an unsuspecting world. The significance of these developments cannot be overstressed because they enabled the raiders and in fact the traders to range far and wide with little to prevent them and with speed and flexibility on their side; they included the introduction of a large mast and broad sail made of wool and reinforced with a diamond stitching pattern, and the introduction of a thicker keel to support this new equipment. The most important element of these developments in respect of raiding was the shallow draught, reconstructions indicate a little over a metre even on large vessels. This was a vital factor for the facility of deep encroachments into the territories of their intended victims, using the shallow creeks and inlets that were inaccessible to ships with deeper hulls. This ability to navigate very shallow stretches of water was a major ingredient in the success of the Vikings both as raiders and merchants.

Modern reconstructions have been attempted by several of the major institutions studying ancient marine technology. Such vessels have been often manned with great competence and success by some major Scandinavian and British living history/battle re-enactment societies. A warship thought to have been known as the Snekkja type (a small vessel 17.5

ritually thrown in rivers. In support of this theory, eight axe-heads were found in the old London Bridge area alone; such great concentrations in rivers and pools would seem to indicate a ritual purpose to their disposal rather than merely battle losses. The fact that in many cases tools, knives and animal bones (which showed no signs of having been butchered for consumption) were found in the same location adds weight to the idea of ceremony rather than of conflict.

Occasional references to axes in the Norse sagas hint at their use as both tools and weapons. In one such tale a warrior called Skarphedin Njalsson jumps across icy waters to reach his enemy while holding his axe above his head. He then lands on the flow and slides towards his enemy so fast that the latter doesn't even have time to put his helmet on before he is dealt a fatal blow to his head, thus, as it says in the saga 'spilling the back teeth onto the ice'. This reference gives such an almost casual account of a Viking's prowess that it seems the axe is almost an extension of his limbs. In another saga, King Olaf's boat builder Thorberg uses his axe to thin down the planks of his famous ship the Long Serpent which was under construction; clearly, Vikings had a variety of uses for metres in length) was reconstructed at the Viking ship museum in Roskilde, Denmark. The original was constructed of oak, ash and deal and indications are that some of the wood had been reused, having been reclaimed from other presumably dismantled or wrecked ships. The theory is that it was built and maintained by local farmers as part of a military obligation, and its size may have limited its range mostly to Baltic waters although a North Sea crossing is not considered to be beyond its ability. The measured performance of the reconstruction indicates a cruising speed of about 6 knots and a maximum speed of 15 knots. The displacement (to include a crew of 30) was 6 tons, and the estimated sail area was 50 square metres; this particular ship was dated to around 1050 A.D. and looking at the surviving material (over 50% of the hull) and the subsequent reconstruction, one can see a strong resemblance to the ships of the essentially Norse warlord Duke William as depicted on the Bayeux tapestry. Such a practical vessel had obviously reached its evolutionary zenith and it would be quite realistic to assume that ships of this type continued to be employed by the Normans as an enduring legacy of their Viking ancestry.

Other developments in Viking shipbuilding included the trimming of parts of the structure to compensate for the added weight of the mast and sails; oar ports were introduced and these were present on the surviving examples of Viking ships from Gokstad (warship, 23 metres long) and Osberg (merchant vessel). Oak and ash were the main materials used to construct these vessels. As an example of Viking engineering, the Gokstad ship's mast was thought to have been over 10 metres high and could be raised and lowered thanks to an ingenious mounting system on the keel. The ships' cables were made from the hides of marine mammals, including whales, seals and walruses, as the Vikings, like the Laplanders, were able to get the most out of the hide by cutting out the cable in a continuous spiral strip. Obviously this provided very tough rigging, and according to one account, ships' cable manufactured by this method could not be broken in a tug of war between 60 men.

Cavalry

Vikings and cavalry do not at first glance seem to fit together, and in the modern imagination they do not have the reputation as mounted warriors enjoyed by their later Norse cousins the Normans. This is a much overlooked aspect of Viking warfare and despite a paucity of archaeological data worth mentioning (apart from several fine examples of richly decorated stirrups found in British rivers), there is sufficient evidence from literary sources to confirm the existence of Viking cavalry.

The first visual images of the role of cavalry in Viking warfare that we come across in this period are the surviving fragments of a tapestry from the Oseberg ship burial (circa 800 A.D.). These fragments clearly show horses drawing wagons and being ridden by warriors. Another piece of evidence for cavalry is the Lewis chesspiece depicting a mounted figure of the later Viking Age; additionally it has the interesting feature of a kite shield and spear.

Ann Hyland in her book *The Mediaeval Warhorse* reports that, according to archaeologists using bone deposits from central Europe, it was with the Germanic and Avar peoples that breeding for heavier horses began in the 9th and 10th centuries; at the same time, horseshoes started to occur in that area. Ann Hyland's opinion is that the shoeing which starts to appear at that time lends force to the increase in size of horses because the heavier body mass coupled

Top.
Coppergate shoe and last. York Archaeological Trust.

Right.
Replica of the Coppergate shoe. Ivor Lawton.

Replica of the Snekkja type (Skudelev 5). This was a small warship. Viking Ship Museum Susan Loyd.

with the weight of an armoured man, and the resulting effect of hard impact with the ground would mean that hooves needed protection from these consequences. Therefore, the indications are that horses available to Vikings would have by no means only been the hardy loadbearing ponies of Scandinavia. The Anglo Saxon Chronicle in 892 A.D. records a Viking raid on the Kent coast where 250 ships landed to engage Alfred's forces which ships were carrying horses that had been stolen from France.

At some point between the end of the 9th and the beginning of the 10th century, a Viking leader of great gifts came to prominence. His name was Hrolf, although his nickname was Gongu-Hrolf, Rolf the Walker, so called because he was presumably too large for a horse to carry. By a strange twist of history, six generations later Hrolf's descendant would be Duke William of Normandy whose successful campaigns hinged on the development of cavalry as a vital part of European warfare.

Normans

Although Norman origins go back to Scandinavia, these Vikings or Northmen, once settled in northern France, did not impose a Norse culture on their new territory and its native peasant inhabitants. Indeed, there is scant evidence from either grave goods or other archaeological finds in Normandy of any co-existing Scandinavian culture. They were open to intermarriage with their Frankish neighbours and indeed with other immigrants from further afield so that it can truly be said by the time of the time of the Conquest the two societies, one Norse, the other Frankish, had merged to create Normans. In fact it is said that the 10th century Duke William Longsword had to send his son, who was to become Richard I, to Bayeux in order to learn Danish.

All of this paints a picture of a people who had evolved into one quite different from the original Viking raiders from whom they were descended, yet an important element of their Scandinavian heritage always remained, and that was their Viking character. It was a Norman trait to use the profits from their war gains to finance further ventures and yet further acquisitions. as well as the establishment of their authority. And in this respect Anna Comnena in the *Alexiad* has this to say about the Norman attitude to wealth, however it was obtained; of Bohemond the Norman, she reports that when he was shown the Byzantine emperor's treasure-house his response was: 'If I had such wealth I would long ago have become master of many lands.' This was the spirit which drove them on to conquer not only England but Sicily, southern Italy and Antioch. A major consitutent of the Viking psyche developed by the Normans was their ability to adapt to and assimilate the native cultures of the lands they had conquered.

The Normans cannot be described as a race in the sense that they have any distinctive racial characteristics, indeed their language was one of the first things to disappear. In the territories of Normandy, Scandinavian roots for place-names are very much in the minority; in most districts of Normandy they are outnumbered by place names which have preserved their Latin roots and such places have Roman remains in abundance, whilst the archaeological evidence for Scandinavian inhabitants is sparse. Fortunately Norman identity did not rest in language, appearance or religion; it was a cultural distinction which hinged on the Norman temperament, itself forged by its Viking ancestry. It is a myth that the Normans were different in their military appearance from their contemporaries; a glance at the sections of the Bayeux tapestry depicting both Saxons and Normans on the field of battle reveals little or no differences in the military equipment of either side. Of course, this may be artistic licence. The artists of the tapestry managed to convey the differences between the two sides by means of hairstyle and other trivial aspects. It is a cause of some frustration for re-enactors of this period that even the most scrupulously authentic late 11th century Saxon may be misapprehended by a public unused to the sight of a Saxon carrying a kite shield; as with all other eras of re-enactment the need for ease of identification and authenticity are often at odds.

Such was the anonymity afforded by the style of armour at this time that incidents like that at the siege of Gerberoi in 1079 were common; Robert of Normandy unhorsed and wounded his own father, William, in the arm, the latter being saved only when his son recognised his voice. A further example of the homogeneity of warrior appearances was that of William the Conqueror having to remove his own helmet during the course of the battle of Hastings to reassure his followers that, despite rumours to the contrary, he was alive. Because of the complications of problems arising due to mistaken identity we can see the start of a system of identification by designs on banner and shield, an embryonic heraldry, as depicted in the Bayeux tapestry; a system which would later form so colourful a part of the medieval battle scene.

The problem facing Norman re-enactors of the period around the time of the battle of Hastings and the years immediately following the conquest, is a lack of archaeological data specific to the area of Normandy or southern England upon which reconstructions can be based. As a result, re-enactment groups such as *Conquest* draw their sources from further afield such as the Low Countries and central Europe as a last resort. This is a reasonable method of tackling the problem if we remember that a significant percentage of the invasion force following William consisted of mercenaries drawn from these and other areas. This would enrich the already diverse pool of military accoutrements and developments available to William for his expeditions. As much as one fifth of William's force did not come from Normandy at all, but from Britanny, Flanders, Artois, Picardy and other places, such as Norman knights from Apulia and Sicily, any of whom in other circumstances might have fought against, rather than with William. Yet by taking part in the expedition to England, these disparate forces bound themselves to William in what many have seen as the birth of a new feudalism, since any lands they gained by force of arms would be his gift and not held in their own names.

All that we have described so far is what has been called *Normanitas*, that is to say, the essence of what it is to be Norman and the Norman's effect on their surroundings. From what has been demonstrated of the Norman culture it is clear that one could be Norman by birth, adoption or fealty; what mattered was to give loyalty to the Norman cause and to share common Norman aspirations. Comparisons between *Normanitas* and its forerunner *Romanitas* have often been made. Indeed a contemporary chronicler said of William at Hastings: 'That he excelled them all both in bravery and soldier craft, so that one might esteem him as at least the equal of the most praised generals of ancient Greece and Rome, he was everywhere battling fearlessly and came to the rescue of many'.

Comparisons can be made with Roman and Norman administration and the equipping of their armies. The contemporary Norman chronicler William of Poitiers indicates the extent of the dominance Duke William exerted over the motley forces that he commanded when he reports that: 'He made generous provision both for his own knights and for those from other parts, but he did not allow any of them to take their sustenance by force. The flocks and herds of the peasantry pastured unharmed throughout the province. The crops waited undisturbed for the sickle without either being trampled by the knights in their pride or ravaged out of greed by plunderers. A weak and unarmed man might watch a swarm of soldiers without fear, and following his horse singing where he would.' Such charismatic leadership, combined with excellent organization of ordnance and provision and the complete compliance of his forces have echoes of the Roman reputation for military order and discipline.

The administration and maintenance of William's army is highlighted in the Bayeux tapestry; large sections given over to portraying the logistical aspect of warfare, such as carts carrying racks of spears and helmets, or the images of mailshirts being carried on yokes following armoured infantry and cavalry, are reminiscent of the 1st century historian Josephus' description of a legion on the march. Whether the same organisation can be attributed to Harold Godwinson's forces is not known, but the depiction of these supply and maintenance units on the Bayeux tapestry rather than merely of scenes of battle and key figures with their weapons can easily be interpreted as an indicator of how the emphasis of Norman and indeed European armies was now shifting from the heroic individual deeds of Dark Age sagas to the practical aims of modern warfare.

Interesting comparisons were made at a recent multi-period re-enactment event, when amongst the many societies lined up for a procession were Roman Legionaries from the end of the 1st century *(Legio II Augusta)*, heavily armoured later Roman troops *(Britannia)* and Norman knights *(Conquest)*. More than one member of the public was to point out the similarities between the three groups in their overall appearance and how the roughly standardised ranks of the late Romans and Normans seemed to echo the glory of Rome. The desire of European rulers to recapture something of Rome's heritage has been demonstrated by the rule of early Germanic kings. A golden seal, thought to have been that of the 9th century Frankish king Charlemagne, is inscribed with the words *Renovatio imperii Romani* – 'for the restoration of Imperial Rome.' In fact, the contemporary chronicler, William of Poitier, the self appointed biographer of Duke William, compares the latter to the military leaders of ancient Rome: 'Marius and Pompey the Great, both of whom earned their victories by courage and ability (since the one brought Jugurtha in chains to Rome whilst the other forced Mithridates to take poison), were so cautious when they were in enemy territory that they feared to expose themselves to danger even by separating themselves with a legion from the main army; their custom was (like that of most generals) to direct patrols and not to lead them. But William, with

Mercenary crossbowmen are paid off, recreated by *Conquest* re-enactment society. Hannah Jenkins.

twenty-five knights and no more, himself went out to gain information about the neighbourhood and its inhabitants. Because of the roughness of the ground he had to return on foot, a matter doubtless for laughter, but if the episode is not devoid of humour it none the less deserves serious praise. For the Duke came back carrying on his shoulder, besides his own hauberk, that of William Fitz-Osbern, one of his companions. This man was famed for his bodily strength and courage, but it was the Duke who relieved him in his necessity of the weight of his armour.'

Helmets

Among the helmets that survive from this period are three particularly fine conicals from central Europe, both are of one piece construction, that is to say they have been beaten from a single sheet of metal. Discussion with modern armourers Roy King and Ivor Lawton reveals that the process of beating a conical helmet out of a single sheet of metal is a difficult task, requiring a great deal of skill and in the Norman era would have needed a large well-run manufacturing

base. The one piece helmet from Olmutz in Moravia (Kunsthistorisches Museum, Vienna) was beaten out of a single sheet of iron and despite its age and surface damage, displays a slight ridge which rises out of the area above a flat and featureless nasal and continues over the peak to terminate at the back of the helmet on the rim. This feature may have been introduced to deflect frontal blows or missile fire. This same feature is to be found on the helmet of St Wenceslas, (Prague Cathedral). This particular helmet has long been associated with the 10th century saint and monarch and is reckoned to be of that date. Unlike the Olmutz helmet, the Wenceslas helmet has an applied thin brow band and an unusually designed combined cross shaped nasal and eybrow component. The Aus der Maas conical (Netherlands, private collection), has been dated to the late 11th, early 12th centuries and was also worked from one sheet of iron and like the Olmutz helmet has an integral nasal which has been sadly damaged. The Aus der Maas helmet has the unusual feature of a heart shaped ring attached to a projection at the peak of the skull area, this can be interpreted as a place to fix a plume or as an aid for carrying, although considering the lack of corroborative pictorial evidence for Norman helmet plumes on sources such as the Bayeux tapestry, the

A great deal of attention is paid to the depiction of the ordnance of William's army on the Bayeux tapestry. Town of Bayeux.

latter option seems more realistic. The Aus der Maas helmet has a curiously broad dome in proportion to its other features, and it has been suggested that the enlarged dome is designed to fit over the head, padding and mail coif of the wearer. The Olmutz and Aus der Maas helmets also share the features of holes around the brow rim which may have supported a lining, mail coif or as suggested by some researchers referring to ambiguous depictions on the Bayeux tapestry; loose leather hoods or applied neck guards. Sadly nothing survives of helmet linings of this era to even suggest how they were padded and fastened but it must be said that the configuration of these brow band holes is similar to modern principals of some military helmet constructions and therefore seems more likely to be a method of securing the lining. Modern re-enactors tend to use a leather webbing device, fabric padded with fleece or just a sheepskin lining glued to the interior of the dome. The other examples worth considering are the quarter braced conicals mentioned in the previous Viking chapter (well represented in earlier and contemporary Viking art as well as in the

Bayeux tapestry) and the long lived segmented *spangenhelm*.

A helmet made from four segments was said to have been found in northern France. It was brought to light by Guy F. Larkin and when first published in his *Record of European Arms and Armour*, the helmet was in a very badly corroded state without a nasal. This was acquired from Lakin by the Bashford Dean Collection of Arms and Armour and sadly restored to the extent that the only useful information left to us was the basic dome construction. In The Bashford Dean exhibition catalogue of 1933 this helmet was described as a 'Conical bowl, 7 and a half inches high, of four segments each 6 inches wide at its base, those of the front and back overlapping the side panels; each joining riveted from the inside by two rivets. The nasal piece is a restoration.'

The Lakin helmet (Metropolitan Museum of Art New York) displays an interesting method of construction which is by no means unique. A Polish helmet (Liverpool Museum) is also composed of four sections, and this has a greater number of rivets which stand proud of the surface in what appears to be a decorative move on the part of the armourer. Much of the gilding survives and traces of applied surface decoration are still present. Helmets represented on the Bayeux tapestry seem to be mostly one or four piece constructions with applied brow bands and nasals. Some manuscript illustrations from this era (the early 12th Century manuscript *St Edmund Routs the Danes* for instance) show what appears to be a strange feature in the apex of many conical domes. These conicals are shown to be kinked or bent forward in the Phrygian cap style, although this has been dismissed by some researchers and armourers as nothing more than artistic fancy. This type of helmet has no archaeological evidence to support its existence but experiments in reconstructions and use on the battlefield have been conducted by Ivor Lawton of *Dawn of Time Crafts* and the Norman re-enactment group *Conquest*. It requires a little more skill and effort to produce a single sheet version, and the resulting form seems to add a little bit more in the way of added strength or deflection properties than a standard conical has to offer.

Body Armour

In this period, the mail hauberk seems to have been the most commonly depicted form of body armour. There is the image of what could be interpreted as a suit of knee length scale armour on the Count of Ponthieu; this has been dismissed by some researchers as patterned or quilted fabric, but the individual leaf shapes and arrangement of this ambiguous element, coupled with its appearance in what is obviously a military situation would, we believe stand on the side of this being a representation of scale. It is worth mentioning that the lack of archaeological evidence for scale armour dated to the conquest era and from the territories held by the Normans means that the policy of many re-enactment societies covering this era is not to use basic scale armour. Visual reference from several sources (the 11th century Italian ivory chesspiece in the shape of a Norman cavalryman) and detail from the ivory cover of Queen Melisende's Psalter) suggests that the Normans used lamellar armour. This ancient style of armour (discussed in the Arthurian chapter) composed of plates or scales that were laced together to form a semi-flexible and highly protective armour, may have been introduced into Norman military society from contact with the Byzantine empire and was thought to have been limited to use by the Normans in their eastern territories of Sicily, Italy and Antioch. The question of

Four section conical helmet said to have been found in Northern France. Metropolitan Museum of Art, New York.

A one piece helmet from Olmutz. Kunshistorishes Museum, Vienna.

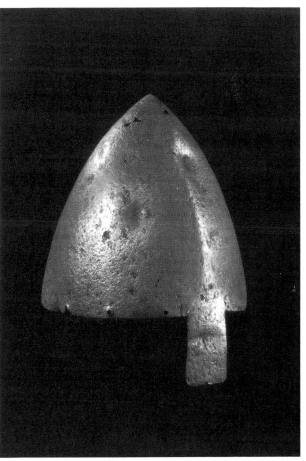

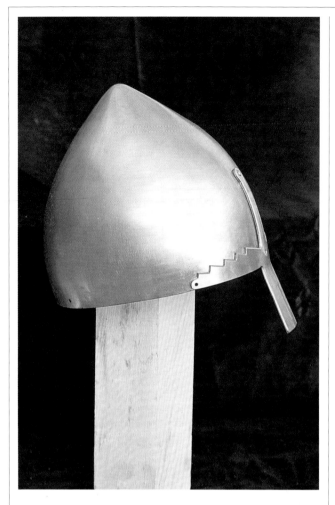

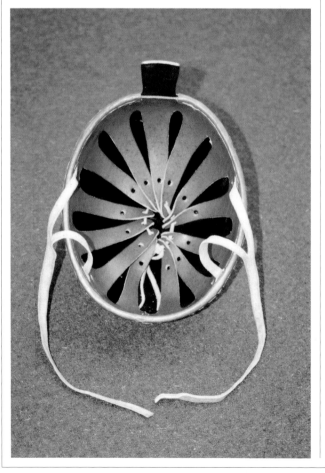

Top left.
Reconstruction of the Wenceslas helmet, made by Ivor Lawton of *Dawn of Time Crafts*.

Top right.
Replica of the Four section conical method, made by Ivor Lawton of *Dawn of Time Crafts*.

Bottom.
Suggested webbing padding of a conical helmet, reconstruction Ivor Lawton of *Dawn of Time Crafts*. John Cole, *Conquest*.

quilted or padded armour in this time has created almost as much controversy as scale, fortunately common sense and the simplicity of construction (quilting in diamond or tube sections of cloth or hide that are then stuffed with straw or fleece) coupled with the undeniable availability of required materials has meant its adoption as an armour in its own right or as padded reinforcement for mail was inevitable. Some visual representations in contemporary manuscripts may be interpreted as padded and quilted armour or just as a stylised technique of representing mail. But we must highlight that two techniques are used to represent armour on the Bayeux tapestry, one area shows four mounted warriors *Milites Festinaverunt Hestingam ut Cibum Raperentur* – ('Soldiers then hurried to Hastings to requisition supplies of food'). Three of these mounted warriors are wearing knee and elbow length hauberks that have been composed of a diamond pattern, the fourth warrior, who appears to be leading the others is wearing a hauberk composed of a pattern of small circles, he is also wearing what appears to have been a coif – this element is absent from the others, so perhaps these differing techniques on the same panel represent different armours, although this is impossible to say with the absence of specific commentary, but the differences are undeniably there. Duke William's half brother Bishop Odo is shown on the Bayeux tapestry to be wearing a battle jacket with an unusual pattern that has been interpreted as both scale or a form of quilted armour. Ringmail seems to have been the principal form of defence of the warrior at the time of the conquest – until recently the representations of armour on the Bayeux tapestry (patterns of large and small rings) were interpreted as large metal hoops that were stitched on to fabric or leather jerkins. The total lack of any archaeological evidence for this style of armour is compounded by the experience of re-

enactors, who agree that this interpretation of the Bayeux hauberk offers little protection of crushing blows and would have offered almost no protection against sharp missiles such as arrows or narrow thrusting spears. It is therefore more likely that the hoop patterns of various sizes are likely to be a representation of ringmail. Ringmail is a flexible and protective surface composed of thousands of tiny iron links that are joined together in a four-through-one pattern, and in most surviving examples the links are often joined and riveted closed like chains, perhaps this prompted the Victorians to give it the epithet 'chain mail'.

Ringmail production even with today's consistent quality and abundant metal supply is a laborious task. Production of ringmail before the industrial era would have been lengthy and expensive, making it the preserve of the warrior élite and the distribution of mailshirts to a significant proportion of an army would have taken a large production base and output on a par with the Roman *fabricae* system in a specific area, not to mention a very large amount of capital. It is likely, considering his inherited wealth and the speed with which his fleet was constructed, that all of these

Replica of the Olmutz helmet, made by Roy King.

Suggested reconstruction of a quarter braced conical helmet.
Chris Lydamore.

elements were within William's capabilities but this is just conjecture. The value of mailcoats is illustrated on the lower section of the Bayeux tapestry as there are numerous illustrations of the dead being stripped of their hauberks. All ringmail reconstructions are heavy to wear, but the weight is fairly evenly distributed, as the shoulders and back of the wearer take most of the strain, and some of the weight can be eased by the wearing of a waist belt; the long mail hauberks of William's army are shown on the Bayeux tapestry as having both elbow and wrist length sleeves, all are knee length and some appear to have the curious feature of a small aperture at the waist in which the sword is slid into a scabbard which sits under the mailcoat's thigh area. Other features include coifs which seem to be both integral and separate to the main mailcoat, and the depiction of a small square of mail on the upper chest area which appears to have a leather or fabric border. This has been interpreted as both doubling on the chest/vital organ area or an open mail face flap or *ventail* that has been left to hang down loose, and in fact several representations in both sculpture and manuscript illustrations from slightly later periods have clear indications of mail flap face guards. We would therefore suggest that the latter option is more likely.

As well as depictions of long mail sleeves there appear to be the first represensions of mail leg defences. Some indications of the weight of Norman mail are given in the Bayeux tapestry, where some of William's men are seen bearing mail on yokes or wooden poles. These poles have been passed through the sleeves of these mail coats, and are depicted as being slightly thicker than the spear shafts on the same tapestry and although depictions of specific proportions and gauges cannot be relied on in this work, the fact that two men are having to bear a loose mailshirt provides some indication of the weight. Many re-enactors choose spring washers, or wire to simulate ringmail, while the more affluent or fortunate have been able to purchase antique Persian or Indian mailshirts at auctions; these are often riveted and butted together, and often, despite their great age they are still every bit as useable as springwasher or wire reconstructions, indicating, we believe, that mailshirts, with maintenance could be used for generations, perhaps centuries.

Swords

As with most Norman equipment from the conquest era we have no surviving swords from a northern French context, but along with many depictions of what could be interpreted as belonging to Scandinavian and Saxon sword types, swords of a distinctly medieval flavour can be clearly seen. Interesting comparisons can be drawn with many of those 'medieval' swords that are featured in the Bayeux tapestry and some central European examples. These have long tapering blades and wide quillions and circular 'pill' or 'Brazil nut' shaped pommels and following the conquest era this seemed to be the direction in which northern European sword technology was to progress. Methods of production and the quality of steel were to improve so that pattern welding was no longer necessary, yet despite these improvements in production it is the authors' opinion that the methods of embellishment that had begun with the Germanic smiths in the late Roman era and reached their zenith in Viking age workshops were in decline; as weapons became more easy to produce they became more functional. This is certainly in evidence in the instances of Norman age scabbard fittings and belt buckles, as surviving copper alloy examples at their most decorative are nowhere near as flamboyant as the examples that would have been worn by their Norse, or Carolingian, ancestors.

Spears

The representations on the Bayeux Tapestry and contemporary manuscripts indicate the use of a variety of spearheads. The Carolingian winged style may be represented in the Norman ranks, and this is quite likely to have been used by them perhaps, as a legacy from both their Scandinavian and Frankish ancestry. The narrow headed thrusting lance is also well represented and many 9th-12th century archaeological examples survive in Europe of both plain and winged headed spears. The barbed 'harpoon' style of spearhead represented on the tapestry has no contemporary archaeological counterpart, and has been dismissed as artistic invention or an alternative renditioning of the Carolingian style spearhead. The spearheads would have been made of iron and, like the swords of this era, less likely to have been decorated in the fashions of earlier Scandinavian and Frankish weaponry, although it is likely as in all conflicts that weapons of antiquity would have found their way onto the battlefield. Spearheads of this and indeed all Dark Age periods would have had hardwood shafts (ash, oak, hornbeam etc) and would have been mostly socketed and fixed with a single rivet to the shaft. These were to play a decisive part in cavalry warfare and will be discussed later in this chapter.

Axes

The great two-handed broad axe of the later Dark

Norman cavalry on the Bayeux tapestry. The Town of Bayeux.

Ages was not the weapon of a cavalryman. This is a fact dictated by practicality rather than protocol or custom, as any seasoned Saxon *huscarl* or Viking re-enactor will testify. The axeman needs to have a firm base to excel in his craft and not the precarious heights of a saddle even with the anchorage of stirrups. One assumes that for this reason the cavalry depicted in the Bayeux Tapestry are not shown to be carrying these great two handed weapons. However there are clear illustrations of a high ranking Norman (the Count of Ponthieu) standing with what is obviously a long-hafted two-handed axe. This has been interpreted as a symbol of high office and may be a legacy of their Norse ancestry, but axes also occur amongst the rank and file of Duke William's army on the tapestry as both tools and weapons.

Another interesting weapon represented on the Bayeux Tapestry is the mace; a Norman is depicted as carrying a version that has a wooden handle with what appears to be a flanged metal head, an interesting footnote as all archaeological examples of this weapon are dated to later periods. One of the contemporary chroniclers describes a Norman cavalryman resorting to a mace as a secondary weapon: 'he raised his shield, and struck one of the Englishmen on the breast, so that iron passed out at his back. At the moment that he fell, the lance broke, and the Frenchman seized the mace that hung on his right side and struck the other Englishman a blow that completely broke his skull...'

Projectile Weapons

There are plenty of visual references to bows on the Bayeux Tapestry, in which these appear to be simple forerunners of the longbow and are likely to have been made of yew. Only one archer is shown as wearing what could be interpreted as a mailcoat, the rest are dressed in simple tunics with quivers suspended from waist belts and are mostly depicted as smaller in size to the key characters; this may have been indicative of their social status. The archers are almost all confined to representation in the the lower border section of the tapestry, and perhaps this was an indication that the archers, like those in English society at the time of Agincourt, were unlikely to have been of noble stock. The surviving arrowheads of this time are predominantly made of iron and socketed, the shapes of arrowhead varying from broad leaf-shaped heads to long narrow square sectioned heads that would have been used for penetrating mail.

Duke William's camp on the eve of the Battle of Hastings, October 13th, 1066.

The main reference for this representation is the Bayeux tapestry. The figures in the foreground, carrying the mailshirt on a pole or yoke along with swords, are taken directly from a section of the tapestry that shows Duke William's army on the march. The mailshirt draped over the yoke has the feature of a padded ventail or face guard, this was thought to have been an integral part of the mailshirt and could be tied up to cover the warrior's mouth and neck. In many cases (as with the mailed figure in the foreground of this representation), the ventail was left open in battle and this feature is thought to have been represented as a leather edged square on the chests of many mailed warriors on the tapestry, and not a square of mail reinforcement (modern reconstructions by re-enactors have revealed that the theory of a mail chest reinforcement is unlikely to be accurate as an extra square of mail on the chest not only inhibits arm movement but also provides little extra protection against impact).

The tunics represented here are based on the tunics represented on the Bayeux tapestry and are likely to have been wool or linen and edged with either embriodery or tablet weaving. The cart is also taken from the Bayeux tapestry and

Norman cavalry at English Heritage re-enactment of Hastings.
Corridors of Time Alan Jeffrey.

carries a barrel, possibly of wine or oil as fresh water would have been readily available from the many streams and rivers in this area of the country. Spears and helmets are also shown and it has been suggested that the conical helmets represented on the tapestry's arms cart may have been stacked on top of each other giving the illusion of being slightly elongated with both a nasal bar and a neck protecting bar. Considering the lack of archaeological evidence for this latter feature it is more likely that the helmets represented here are just stacked on top of each other.

The armoured figure (top left) talking to the central figure of Duke William is wearing a knee and elbow length mailshirt that is divided up the middle for movement and for riding. His helmet is based on a segmented example found in Northern France and now in the Metropololitan Museum of Art in New York, however the brow band on the helmet is an artistic addition (a realistic fusion of the archaeological example and representation of similar helmets on the Bayeux tapestry). The methods by which the kite shields were gripped are taken from contemporary and slightly later manuscript illustrations as no archaeological examples survive.

The swords themselves are based on contemporary European swords. Blades in the 11th century were becoming longer and tapering down to sharp points, the elongated cross guards and tablet or Brazil-nut pommels were likely to have been iron, and surviving examples are mostly undecorated and **very functional in appearance.** Painting by Richard Hook.

The Crossbow

There is certainly evidence for crossbows in Britain before the Norman Conquest, as we have discussed in the earlier chapter on the Picts. As these early crossbows relied on prods made of ash or yew for power, the velocity cannot have been as great as later versions that used metal for prods. Crossbows are strangely absent from the Bayeux Tapestry, although this absence has been suggested to be the result of a Papal decree rather than a verdict of their ability as a weapon. Their effectiveness in this era should not be doubted when the reader considers this early 12th century account from the Byzantine princess Anna Comnena who refers to the crossbow as being 'the bow of the barbarians and goes on to describe its effectiveness in detail: 'In the middle of the string is a socket, a cylindrical kind of cup fitted to the string itself and about as long as an arrow of considerable size which reaches from the string to the very middle of the bow, and through this arrows of many sorts are shot out. The arrows used with this bow are very short in length, but very thick, fitted in front with a heavy iron tip. And in discharging them the string shoots them out with enormous violence and force, and whatever these darts hit, they do not fall back, but they pierce through the shield, then cut through a heavy iron corslet and wing their way through and out the other side.'

Despite a total absence of crossbows on the Bayeux Tapestry, William of Poitiers refers to Duke William using them. There is also the account of the battle from Guy de Amiens who refers to *Ballistantes* but these can equally be interpreted as slingers and are certainly featured on the tapestry, and of course Guy himself is not as reliable a source as Poitiers.

The growing ability to produce consistent tempering of iron following the Conquest was not only employed on sword blades but used to produce metal crossbow prods as this 'bow of the barbarians' needed to improve to compete with developments in body armour. As larger areas of metal plate were used in the defence against missile fire, weapons were judged on their ability to penetrate this.

Shields

The most commonly featured shield on the Bayeux

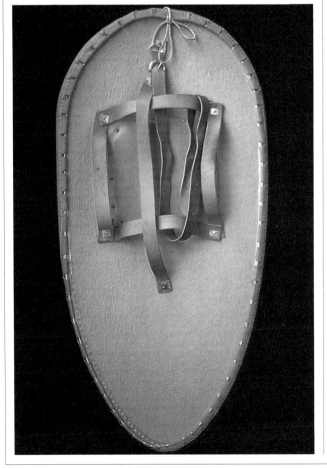

Tapestry is the 'kite shield', this is often mistakenly referred to as the 'Norman shield' although just as much emphasis is given to it in the ranks of the Saxon *huscarls* depicted on the Bayeux Tapestry and the evidence shows that it certainly occurs in other European cultures before the Conquest period. No kite shields survive to the present day, but we are left with enough visual evidence and contemporary archaeological data from which to create convincing reconstructions. The first consideration has to be to the effectiveness of the reconstructions of the kite shield in battle re-enactment, and the advantages of using a kite shield as a cavalryman are immediately obvious. The Bayeux Tapestry and modern recreations reveal that kite shields give the horseman almost total protection on one flank, as the downward point of the shield covers the rider's entire leg on one side and there is also significantly less weight than with an obtuse oval or round shield of a similar size. This weight factor meant that the point of the shield could be used offensively as well as defensively, a fact that seems to be corroborated by William of Poitiers' account of Duke William's personal valour at Hastings 'not a few felt the weight of his shield' and further

supported by figures on the Bayeux Tapestry who seem to be leading with the point of their shields. From the experience of using a large uniform infantry unit of kite shields at a re-enactment of the Battle of Hastings, the arrangement of the grip straps seemed to vary according to the individual's ability and preference; some chose to grip with their arms facing down towards the point (a style of grip that assisted the ability to punch with the point), whereas some chose to have their forearms gripping the inside of the shield at a 45 degree upward facing angle (increasing the wearer's ability to parry blows and defensive ability against falling missile fire). This discrepancy of grip arrangements is quite historically accurate, as the Bayeux Tapestry clearly shows several styles of differing grip strap arrangements; the ability to maintain a solid shield wall is not as effective with kite shields that do not have uniform methods of gripping. A French shield wall formation illustrated on the *Apocalypse of St Sever* (mid-late 11th century) shows the shields to be held at differing angles, leaving large areas of their bodies exposed and vulnerable. However the image on the Bayeux Tapestry of Saxon *huscarls* on Senlac hill shows a uniform and tight shield wall composed of kite shields, perhaps displaying a uniform

Modern mail shirt reproduction, by Ivor and Simone Lawton, *Dawn of Time Crafts*.

Norman swords. Hannah Jenkins *Conquest*.

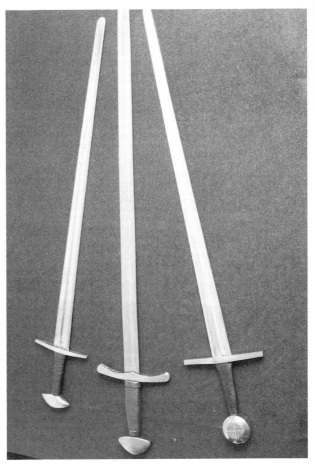

Suggested reconstruction of the 'Phrygian cap' style helmet, by Ivor Lawton of *Dawn of Time Crafts*.

Recreated Norman infantryman in a padded 'quilted' jacket.

Hannah Jenkins *Conquest*.

method of gripping the kite shield amongst Harold's bodyguard, although a 'square' arrangement of straps on the reverse of one of the Bayeux shields may be an indication of a universal grip, allowing the warrior to hold his kite shield in a variety of ways. The use of a large central boss covering a gripping handle is unnecessary on a kite shield and kite shield bosses represented in contemporary art tend to appear too tiny to protect a gripping hand, and would therefore be most likely to be decorative.

An 11th-12th century find from Switzerland supports the use of small bosses as decorative features at this time. This tiny object is made of copper alloy and was gilded, and the flange has been cut into a decorative pattern and has four small rivet holes, the total diameter, including flange is 7.2cm, far too small to protect an adult's hand. We have no surviving archaeological data on the shield body and can only speculate to its reconstruction, whether planking or plywood; the materials are likely to have been ash, oak or lime, and it could have been covered in fabric and or leather and painted, and the edging could have been rawhide although some surviving contemporary

exterior shield mounts are copper alloy.

Cavalry Warfare

Norman military excursions almost always depended on their mounted forces. Norman cavalry was used with great effect in their campaigns not only at Hastings but also in other parts of France and as far as Italy, Syria and Byzantium. Cavalry as a military tool is unlike any other because its success was not just due to its inherent power to strike but in its feudal connection. Cavalry and the feudal system went hand in hand and as we have seen, the Normans were the chief pioneers of this system. The feudal system was based in part on the possession of land for horses to be reared on or purchased from the profits of its cultivation. By the 11th century the horse was highly prized, a possession on a par with landholding.

Today, the Norman partnership with its cavalry seems indissoluble; indeed, according to the Carolingian chronicles and Lot's *L'Art Militaire* it was only once the Norsemen had set foot on the Frankish and Breton soil of Northern France that they began to exchange their tradition of sea raiding for horseback incursions and assaults in order to make rapid and efficient forays into the French countryside. By the early 10th century these proto-Normans had settled in various regions of northern France and the age of the Norman with its emphasis on horse warfare had begun.

By settling in the lands of the Carolingian empire, they took over an already established tradition of horse breeding from the west Franks, the royal Frankish annals in the Carolingian chronicles give many accounts of the use of cavalry in conflicts through the late 8th to early 9th century, and they also document methods of horse rearing and management. Due to the wide ranging nature of their cavalry campaigns, they were subject to the influences of mounted opponents, most notably the Muslims through whom Arab blood stock was introduced into the more mundane steeds of western Europe. In fact, so impressed were the Franks when they encountered Moorish cavalry that they were persuaded to place a far greater emphasis on cavalry than infantry. There is no doubt that the introduction of Arabian bloodlines improved the pool of horse supplies in Europe

Bottom left and right.

Interpretations of ventails (ringmail face covering in a slightly later side flap method). Conquest. Hannah Jenkins.

generally, this seems to have been the case particularly in Spain, so that by the time of the battle of Hastings, Duke William's warhorse, a gift from King Alfonso of Leon, is recorded as having been brought out of Spain by Walter Giffard. This is recorded by Wace in his *Roman de Rou*.

Although we have no records of the exact type or confirmation of the horses used by the Normans, the Bayeux Tapestry gives some idea as to the build of the horses brought over to England for the invasion. However, it must be remembered that the Normans were as well aware of the need for different types of horse for different tasks as any other horse orientated military powers of that time. Of course, the warhorse as we think of it had not yet become the load bearing heavy horse, or destrier, of the later medieval accounts. An interesting guide to the size of the horses used by the Normans is provided by examination of finds of Norman horseshoes. Ann Hyland in her book *The Medieval Warhorse*, measured some of the surviving Norman horseshoe examples and found that one set of Norman shoes measured exactly the same as a modern Arabian mare of 15.1 hands. Her opinion on the basis of these findings and measurement was that the Norman horses could not have been of any great weight as hooves of corresponding size would not be able to carry the burden of a heavy horse. She goes on

Different ways to grip a kite shield.

to suggest that the hooves were 'more closely akin to an animal in the region of 800 to 1000 lbs (360-455 kg). Such an animal is able to carry considerable weight.'

Concentrating on the Norman invasion of England, where cavalry was very much to the fore, the achievement of the transportation of over 2,000 warhorses by ship across the channel is not an inconsiderable one. It was here that the traditional Norse ship building skills were undoubtably used as the ships featured on the Bayeux Tapestry can testify. The Norman fleet appears to have consisted of more than one type of vessel, and it is a matter of conjecture as to whether the ships that provided horse transport were warships with shallow drafts or larger warships with deeper drafts allowing for the stalling of horses below decks and the consequent disembarkation by ramp.

The feat of ferrying such large numbers of chargers, not to mention their fodder, horse gear and grooms is one which had to overcome many obstacles. It is quite probable that lessons in the art of horse transportation had been learnt by the Normans during their Sicilian campaigns (1060-1061). Certainly

William's invasion force included knights from Apulia and Sicily, mercenaries from those campaigns, and it is reasonable to assume that their advice on the construction and practice of horse transportation would have been very valuable to Duke William when planning the expedition.

The Bayeux Tapestry itself depicts horses jumping directly from the ships into shallow water without the aid of ramps, but it would be dangerous to assume that this reflected the actual process of horse disembarkation, as it may well be an artistic device although the artist has taken some trouble to indicate that the horses came ashore unaided by depicting the left hind leg of a horse still on board, whilst the animal itself has jumped into the shallows. An interesting experiment in horse transportation was conducted in 1963 when some Danish scouts used a replica of the 9th century Ladby ship, a ship of extremly shallow draft, to demonstrate how horses could be jumped from the low side of the ship from the low side of a ship into shallows or a quay side. Unfortunately the ship and its equine cargo were never tested in an open sea crossing; the weight and unpredictability of the horses on board would most probably have rendered a ship of such shallow draft quite unstable and does not therefore seem very practical. Bearing in mind the nature of the English Channel, a waterway prone to storms and unexpected wind changes, coupled with the many difficulties with transporting live animals, it is hardly surprising that Duke William changed the fleet's point of departure from the Dives estuary and surrounding harbours to the mouth of the Somme. The shorter sea crossing from the Somme would have had many advantages, not least that of a less adverse affect on the horses' condition, an important consideration in a military system where the knights expected to get ashore and be ready for battle almost immediately. As already discussed, 2,000 warhorses came ashore with Duke William's invasion force. It is easy to imagine what effect such a large contingent of cavalry would have had on the minds of the Saxon force as in 1990 and 1995 at re-enactments of the battle of Hastings on the site of the original conflict, when less than 30 Norman cavalry was used on the first occasion (and around 50 on the second) to great effect.

As important as the quality of the mounts was the comfort and security of the equipment of both man and horse. We have already discussed how Carolingian cavalry advances had been passed on to the Normans and in respect of saddles there is an interesting depiction in the St Gallen Psalter of the late 9th-early 10th century, which shows saddles of the Carolingian horse with distinct similarities, particularly in the pommel and cantle heights, to famous horned saddles depicted on Roman monuments. The St Gallen saddle also has stirrups. So it is reasonable to assume that this type of saddle may have contributed to the development of the Norman saddle as used at Hastings. The Bayeux Tapestry is our best evidence for Norman saddles at Hastings; those depicted are shown almost without exception as having very high pommels and cantles. Occasionally the cantle is shown as being slightly higher than the pommel. The saddles have girths and of course stirrups which are worn long and placed further forward on the saddle than is usual nowadays. It has been suggested that this stirrup placement had the effect of causing the rider to stand in his stirrups rather than sitting deep in the saddle, this in turn would enable him to brace himself to drive his lance or sword with greater power. One disadvantage to the high pommel and cantle was that stopping abruptly from a fast pace or sudden unexpected movements could result in injury to the rider from the pommel or cantle as was thought to have happened to William the Conqueror himself, when after the sack of Mantes (northern France 1087), his horse, frightened by debris from the burning city, shied or stumbled and threw William violently against the high saddle pommel. Some attribute his consequent severe intestinal pains and death shortly after to an internal rupture caused by this incident.

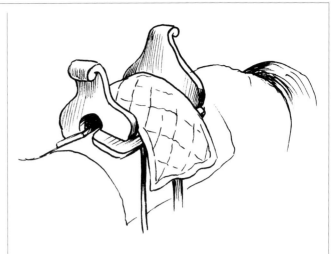

High Norman saddle.

Decorative copper-alloy boss from Switzerland 11th-12th century.

Bibliography

Primary source

Ammianus Marcellinus, *The Later Roman Empire* (Tran. W. Hamilton), Penguin Classics, 1986.

Aneirin, *Y Gododdin* (Tran. A, O, H, Jarman) The Welsh Classics, Gomer Press, 1990.

Beowulf, *A Verse Translation* (Tran. M. Alexander), Penguin Classics, 1973.

The Earliest English Poems (Tran. M. Alexander), Penguin Classics, 1966.

Gildas (*Arthurian Period Sources* Vol.7, Dr John Morris), Phillimore, 1978.

The Mabinogion (Tran. G. Jones and T. Jones), Everyman, J.M. Dent, 1979.

Nennius (*Arthurian Period Sources* Vol.8, Dr John Morris & Mrs S. Morris), Phillimore, 1980.

St. Patrick, (*Arthurian Period Sources* Vol.9, Dr John Morris), Phillimore, 1978.

Procopius, *History of the Wars* (Tran. H.B. Dewing), Loeb Classical Library, 1914.

Procopius, *The Secret History* (Tran. G.A. Williamson), Penguin Classics, 1966.

Tacitus, *On Britain and Germany* (Tran. H. Mattingly), Penguin Classics.

The Tain (Tran. T. Kinsella), Oxford University Press, 1969.

Vegetius, *Epitome of Military Science* (Tran. N.P. Milner) Liverpool University Press, 1993.

Secondary Works

Alcock , L, *Arthur's Britain*, Pelican Books, 1971

Allason-Jones, L, *Women in Roman Britain*, British Museum Publications, 1989.

Allen-Brown, R, *The Normans*, Boydell Press, 1984.

Berg, M, & Litvinoff, *Ancestors – The Origins of the People and the countries of Europe*, Peter Lowe, 1992.

Berresford Ellis, P, *Celt & Saxon, The Struggle for Britain A.D. 410-937*, Constable, 1993.

Berresford Ellis, P, *A Guide to Early Celtic Remains in Britain*, Constable, 1991.

Bishop, M.C. & Coulston, *Roman Military Equipment,* B.T. Batsford, 1993.

Campbell, B, *The Roman Army 31B.C. - A.D. 337, A Sourcebook*, Routledge, 1994.

Campbell, J, *The Anglo-Saxons*, Penguin Books, 1982.

Cruickshank, G, *The Battle of Dunnichen*, The Pinkfoot Press, 1991.

Davis, R.H.C, *The Normans and their Myth*, Thames and Hudson, 1976.

Dent, A & Goodhall, D.M., *A History of British Native Ponies*, J.A. Allen, 1962.

Douglas, D.C., *William the Conqueror*, Eyre Methuen, 1964.

Evans, A.C., *The Sutton Hoo Ship Burial*, British Museum Publications, 1986.

Frere, S, *Britannia*, Pimlico, 1991.

Gravett, C, *Hastings 1066, The Fall of Saxon England*, Osprey Campaign Series, 1992.

Hall, R, *Viking Age York*, English Heritage (B.T. Batsford), 1991.

Harrison, M, *Anglo-Saxon Thegn 449-1066A.D.*, Osprey Warrior Series, 1993.

Harrison, M, *Viking Hersir 793-1066 A.D.*, Osprey Warrior Series, 1993.

Hyland, A, *Equus- The Horse in the Roman World*, B.T. Batsford, 1990.

Hyland, A, *The Medieval Warhorse, From Byzantium to the Crusades*, Sutton Publishing, 1994.

Hills, C, *The Blood of The British*, George Philip & Ch4, 1986.

Holder, P.A, *The Roman Army in Britain*, B.T. Batsford, 1982.

Johnson, S, *Roman Fortifications on the Saxon Shore*, Dof E and H.M.S.O., 1977.

Laing, J & L, *Celtic Britain and Ireland-The Myth of the Dark Ages*, Irish Academic Press, 1990.

Laing, J & L, *The Picts and the Scots*, Alan Sutton, 1993.

Macdowall, S, *Germanic Warrior*, Osprey Warrior Series, 1996.

Macdowall, S, *The Late Roman Infantryman*, Osprey

warrior Series, 1994.

Mack, A, *Field Guide to the Pictish Symbol Stones*, Pinkfoot Press, 1996.

Morris, Dr J, *The Age of Arthur*, Phillimore, 1973.

Newark, T, *Celtic Warriors*, Blandford Press, 1986.

Newark, T, *The Barbarians-Warriors and Wars of the Dark Ages*, Blandford Press, 1985.

Nicholle, D. (PhD), *Arthur and the Anglo-Saxon Wars*, Osprey Men at Arms Series.

Nicholle, D. (PhD), *Romano-Byzantine Armies 4th-9th Centuries*, Osprey Men at Arms Series.

Phillips, G, & Keatman, M, *King Arthur the True Story*, Arrow books 1992.

Rhanders, Pehrson J, *Barbarians and Romans*, BCA, 1983.

Richards, J.D. *Viking Age England*, B.T. Batsford, 1991.

Rivet, A.L.F. Smith, C, *The Place Names of Roman Britain*, Batsford, 1979.

Rud, M, *The Bayeux Tapestry and the Battle of Hastings 1066*, Christian Eilers, 1983.

Scullard, H.H, *Roman Britain Outpost of the Empire*, Thames and Hudson, 1979.

Seagroat, M, *Coptic Weaves*, Merseyside County Council Publication.

Southern, P & Dixon, K.R, *The Late Roman Army*, B.T. Batsford, 1996.

Southern, P & Dixon, K.R, *The Roman Cavalry*, B.T. Batsford, 1993.

Sutherland, E, *In search of the Picts*, Constable, 1994.

Thurlow Leeds, E, *The Archaeology of the Anglo-Saxon Settlements*, Oxford University Press, 1913.

Webster, L. & Brown, M, *The Transformation of the Roman World*, British Museum Press, 1997.

Welch, M, *Anglo-Saxon England*, English Heritage (B.T. Batsford), 1992.

Wernick, R, *The Vikings- The Seafarers*, Time Life Books.

Wild, J.P, *Textiles in Archaeology*, Shire Archaeology, 1988.

Wilkinson, D. & Cantrell J, *The Normans in Britain*, Macmillan, 1987.

Wilson, R.J.A. *A Guide to the Roman Remains in Britain*, Constable, 1975.

Wood, M, *In Search of the Dark Ages*, BBC Books, 1981.

Archaeological Reports & Specialist Information

Colchester Archaeological Report 2: The Roman Small Finds from Excavations in Colchester 1971-79, Nina Crummy.

North Shoebury: Settlement and Economy in South East Essex 1500BC- AD 1500, J.J. Wymer & N.R. Brown.

Spong Hill, Catalogue of Inhumations (Part III) Norfolk Museums Service 1984, C. Hills, K. Penn, R. Rickett.

Recent Research in Archaeological Footwear
Edited by: D. E. Friendship Taylor, B.A.
        J.M. Swann, MBE., B.A., F.M.A.
        S.Thomas, B.A., Dip. Cons A.M.A.
        Association of Archaeological Illustrators & Surveyors
        In association with the Archaeological Leather Group.

Excavations of Forts on the Portalloch Estate, Argyll, Proc Soc Antiq Scot 39, 1904-05.

Excavations on Iona 1979, John W. Barber, Proc Soc Antiq Scot, 111, 1981, 282-380.

Anglo Saxon Shields, Tania Dickinson & Heinrich Harke.

Dark Ages Directory

Re-enactment Societies

(S.A.E. Appreciated in all cases).

Britannia (Later Roman & 5th Century Arthurian Re-enactment and Living History), 13 Ardleigh, Basildon, Essex SS16 5RA.

The Swords of Pedragon (5th Century Arthurian Re-enactment), 1 Hazel Way, Shrublands Estate, Gorleston, Great Yarmouth, Norfolk NR31 8LP.

Venta Silurum 456 (5th Century Arthurian Re-enactment), 18 Sandy Lane, Caldicot, Monmouthshire NP6 4NA.

The Wulfingas Society (Early Saxon Settlement, Re-enactment and Living History), 35a Bank Street, Brampton, Chesterfield S40 1BH.

Milites Litoris Saxonici (Germanic mercenaries in the later Roman Army, Living History), 82 London Road Faversham, Kent ME 13 8TA.

Conquest (Norman era Re-enactment and Living History), 61 King Edward's Grove, Teddington, Middlesex TW 11 9LZ.

N.F.P.S. (The Vikings, Re-enactment and living history), 119 Market St, Broadley, Whitworth, Rochdale Ol12 8SE.

Regia Anglorum (Later Saxon era Re-enactment and living history), 9 Durleigh Close, Headly Park, Bristol BS13 7NQ.

The Free Company (Variety of time periods- Celt, Dark Age and Mediaeval), 19 Down Terrace, Brighton, East Sussex BN2 2ZJ.

Brega (5th-7th Century Irish Warriors), 94 West Street, Drogeda, County Louth, Eire.

An Dul Cuinn Clan (Variety of time eras of historic Ireland), Clan Resource Centre, Dublin 11.

Related period societies

Brigantia (Iron Age Celts, Re-enactment and living History), 67 Paulsgrove Road, North End, Portsmouth, Hampshire PO2 7HP.

The Silures (Iron Age Celts) 20 Mendip View, Wick, Bristol, BS15 5PY.

The Ermine Street Guard (1st-2nd Century Roman Living history and Display), Oakland Farm, Dog Lane, Crickley Hill, Witcombe, Gloucester GL3 4UG.

Legio VIII AUGUSTA (1st-2nd Century Roman Living History and Display), 31 Llwyn Menlli, Ruthin, Clwd, Wales Ll15 1RG.

Legio II AUGUSTA (1st-2nd Century Roman Living History and Display), 288 Copnor Road, Copnor, Portsmouth, Hampshire PO3 5DD.

Medieval Siege Society (Also supplier of Longbows and Archery equipment), 70 Markyate Road, Dagenham, Essex RM8 2LD.

The White Company (Medieval Battle Re-enactment and living History), 77 Stokefield, Pitsea, Basildon, Essex SS13 1NJ.

Medieval Combat Society, Flat 2, 93 Surbiton Road, Kingston, Surrey KT1 2HW.

Armourers, Craftspeople and Re-enactment services

Ivor and Simone Lawton (*Dawn of Time Crafts*, Armour, weapons and living history items, from Bronze age to Medieval), 18 Anne Close, Brightlingsea, Essex CO7 0LS.

A. E. Mason (Weyland Iron, buckles & brooches, Roman to medieval), 176 Victoria St, Hartshill, Stoke on Trent ST4 6HD.

Ben Levick (*Bodgit & Bendit*, Replica artefacts from Ancient times to the Middle Ages), c/o The cellar, 2 Prospect row, Old Brompton, Gillingham, Kent ME7 5AL.

Corridors of Time (Specialist personnel & props to cover most historical periods for presentation or filmwork), Alan Jeffrey, 11 Mulberry Court, Pagham, W. Sussex PO21 4TP (01243 262291).

Armourclass (Swords), 193 (a) Dumbarton Road, Clydebank, Glasgow.

Peter Faulkner Coracles, 24 Watling Street, Leintwardine, Shropshire SY7 OLW.

Ancestral Instruments (Musical Instruments from Ancient to Victorian), David Marshall, Tudor Lodge, Pymoor Lane, Pymoor, Ely, Cambridgeshire CB6 2EE.

Tidr Axholmr Butsekarlborg (Viking Living History) 15 Mond Avenue, Goole, East York DN14 6LQ.

Anne Laverick (Cloth Supplier & National Organiser of the Re-enactor's Market), Vale Head Farm, Knottingley, West Yorkshire, WF 11 8RN.

Tim Noyes (Swords & Helmets), 46 Eddington Lane, Herne Bay, Kent CT6 5TS.

Victor James (Tent Maker), Anglesey Road, Burton on Trent, Staffordshire DE14 3NE.

Saxon Village Crafts, Delbush, Whatlington Road, Battle, East Sussex, TN33 0JN.

Bows (See the Medieval Siege Society in previous section).

Uncle Matt's Scale Armour (Variety of scales for armour), c/o Britannia, 13 Ardleigh, Basildon, Essex.

Green Tools (Tools and cookery equipment), 47 Kingston Road, Camberley, Surrey GU15 4AG.

Historical societies and publications

CALL TO ARMS (Directory of British and Worldwide Re-enactment Societies and Craftspeople covering Bronze Age to the Present era), Duke Henry Plantagenet, Main office: 7 Chapmans Crescent, Chesham, Buckinghamshire HP5 2QU.

The Pictish Arts Society, 27 George Square, Edinburgh, EH8 9LD.

The Pinkfoot Press (publishers specialising in early Scottish, Irish and Manx history), c/o David Henry, The Pinkfoot Press, Balgavies, (by Forfar) Angus, Scotland DD8 2TH.

The Battlefield Press (publications on Battlesites), 34 Greenfields, Heckmondwike, West Yorkshire WF16 9HG.

Museums

The British Museum, Russell Square, London. Early Medieval room houses the largest collection of 3rd century A.D. to 1100 A.D. artefacts in the world (this includes the Sutton Hoo find and re-constructions).

Caerleon Roman Fortress (B4326 North of Newport, Wales).

Worth a vist, the Baths, Amphitheatre and parts of the Fortress are well preserved and presented by Cadw (Welsh Historic Monuments).

The Roman Legionary Museum, Caerleon, Gwent, Wales.

Lindisfarne Priory and Museum, Holy Island, Northumbria (English Heritage).

Sheffield City Museum, Weston Park, Sheffield (Anglo Saxon section houses the Benty Grange helmet).

Dover Museum, Market Square, Dover, Kent (covering Dover's history as a Roman port and displaying finds from a local Anglo-Saxon cemetary).

Norwich Castle Museum, Norwich, (Norfolk Museums service),

Fine collection of Iron Age Celtic, Roman, Saxon and Norman artefacts.

Kings Lynn Museum, Kings Lynn, (Norfolk Museums Service), Iron-Age Celtic, Later Roman and Saxon artefacts and re-constructions.

Swaffham Museum, Swaffham, Norfolk, artefacts and displays dealing with Swaffham's origins as a town towards the end of the Roman Empire (displays vary).

Jorvik Viking Centre, York, Viking living history displays and a reconstructed settlement in the Museum.

Museum of London, London wall, covering London's human habitation from the Stone Age to the present.

Royal Museum of Scotland and Museum of Antiquities, Queen Street, Edinburgh, Scotland, from pre-history to the present.

National Museum of Ireland, Kildare Street, Dublin 2, from pre-history to the present.

If you want to visit an English Heritage site on the day of an historical re-enactment then contact the English Heritage Special Events Department (0171- 973 3000) or write to them at; 429 Oxford Street W1R 2HD.

Models and Wargaming Suppliers

Simon J. Oliver (*Guardsroom minatures*) supplier and painter of Ancient to Medieval figures, concentrating on Britain's Dark Age. 3 Station Avenue, Prittlewell, Southend-on-Sea, Essex SS2 5ED.

Index

Acknowledgements

We would like to thank the following people for their help on this book; Ivor and Simone Lawton (for hours of your valuable time and advice, allowing us to use your work and a great dinner). John Eagle, Alan Jeffrey of *Corridors of Time*, A.E. Mason (*Weyland Iron*), Russell Scott (N.F.P.S.), Paul & Penny Lydiate (N.F.P.S.), Dr Glenys Lloyd Morgan F.S.A. Mike & Carole Hardy (Swaffham Museum), Ted & Rosemary Batterham, Fraser Hunter (National Museums of Scotland), Mark Harrison, Dr G. Cruickshank, David Henry and all at Pinkfoot Press, T.E. Gray, Peter Connolly F.S.A., Derek Edwards, Dave Wicks (Norfolk Museums Service, Landscape Photography), Peter Faulkner (Coracle maker), Ben Levick (of Bodgit & Bendit Ltd), John Cole and all in *Conquest*, Howard Giles, Thomas Cardwell and Mike Brown (English Heritage Special Events Dept), Mark Griffin (*The White Company*), Kim Siddorn (*Regia Anglorum*), Phil Fraser (*Medieval Siege Society*), Roy King, Prof. George Bass (Institute of Nautical Archaeology- Texas), Nikolai Tolstoy, Nick Fuentes (Roman Army Research Society of London), John Harris, Dylan, Tim Noyes and Julian(and all in *Milites Litoris Saxonici*), Fiona from *Seventh Art Productions*, Phil Prentis, Brian Heggarty, Jo Hurley, Shelagh Simpson, John Nash, Pete Seymour (*Saemarr*), Bernard Jacobs, The Royal Armouries (Tower of London), British Museum (Kate Down), Kings Lynn Museum, Norwich Castle Museum, Nick and Pat Nethercoat, Iain Bell, Matt Shadrake, Chris Sycamore, Ian Burridge, Mandy Turner, Gary Lee, Scotsman Publications, York Archaeological Trust, Sheffield City Museum, Derek & Maureen Clow, The Metropolitan Museum of Art (New York), Andy Palmer, Nick Ansell, Robin Woosey and Maxine Clarke, Steve Camp, The Kunshistorisches Museum (Austria), The 'Centre Guillaume Conquerant' of Bayeux, Eamon and Peta Shaw, Anthony Farrow, Justin Ruth, Glen Lovelock, Steven Wade, Penny Gillison, Steve Morris, Phil Budd, Gary Foreland, Geoff Maynard, Jim Allabush, Chris Pegley, Magical Dave, Stuart Klatcheff, Museum of London, Chris Haines (*Ermine St Guard*), Brian Dowling, Mandy Hammond, Jeff Brimble (*VIII Augusta*), Mike & Angie Day (*Venta Silurum*), D. Holman (*Swords of Pendragon*), Cadw (Welsh Heritage), The Viking Ship Museum in Demark and a special thank you to our dear friend Lynne Smith. Thanks also to Tim Newark at *Military Illustrated*.